Collins

South Downs Park Rangers Favourite Walks

National Parks | SOUTH DOWNS NATIONAL PARK

Published by Collins
An imprint of HarperCollins*Publishers*
Westerhill Road, Bishopbriggs, Glasgow G64 2QT
collins.reference@harpercollins.co.uk
www.harpercollins.co.uk

HarperCollins*Publishers*
1st Floor, Watermarque Building, Ringsend Road, Dublin 4, Ireland

Printed in China by RR Donnelley APS Co Ltd

ISBN 978-0-00-843911-8 10 9 8 7 6 5 4 3 2 1

MIX
Paper from responsible sources
FSC™ C007454

This book is produced from independently certified FSC™ paper to ensure responsible forest management.

For more information visit: www.harpercollins.co.uk/green

Contents

WALK LOCATIONS

▼ Recommended starting point for each route – refer to individual walk instructions for more details.

WALK 20
Amberley,
page 122

WALK 2
Devil's Dyke,
page 24

WALK 5
Hamsey,
page 40

WALK 11
Lewes and Glynde,
page 72

WALK 16 **Alfriston and the Cuckmere Valley,** *page 98*

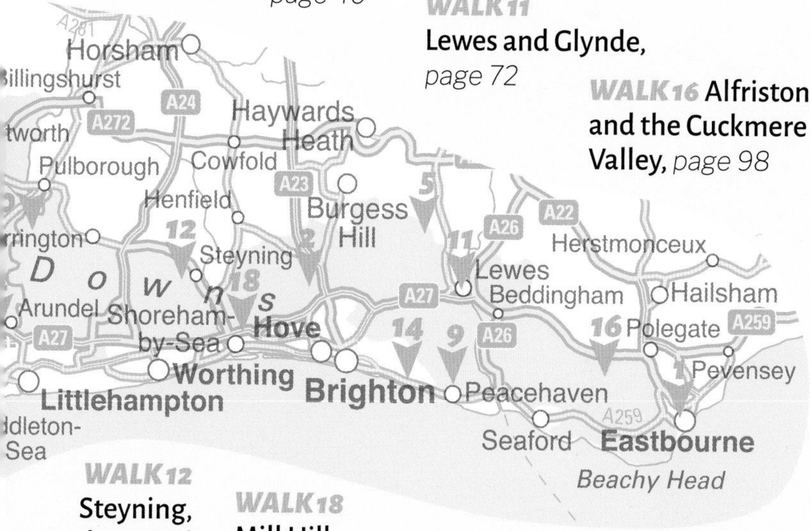

WALK 12
Steyning, Chanctonbury and Washington,
page 78

WALK 18
Mill Hill,
page 110

WALK 14
Rottingdean,
page 90

WALK 9
Telscombe and Mill Hill,
page 62

WALK 1
Sussex Heritage Coast, *page 18*

With over 2,000 miles of public rights of way, the National Park offers opportunities for walkers at all levels, from a gentle afternoon stroll to a long-distance hike.

Introduction

The South Downs National Park has it all: rolling hills, magical heathland, stunning river valleys, ancient woodland, thriving villages and market towns, and the iconic white chalk cliffs of the Sussex Heritage Coast.

England's third largest National Park is also its youngest, having celebrated the tenth anniversary of its creation in 2020.

Occupying over 600 square miles of lush green lowland within the UK's busiest region, there is a timeless appeal to the park's gentle landscape. Here, in the sunniest part of the country, sun-kissed vineyards produce some of Britain's best sparkling wines, and people come together in low-beamed pubs and at country fairs to enjoy what the area has to offer.

The grassy-topped wave of hills that gives the park its name is truly magnificent, but the South Downs National Park extends beyond the Downs to include the woodlands, hedgerows and lowland pastures of the Western Weald, as well as several beautiful rivers.

Around a quarter of the park is covered with trees, making this the most wooded National Park in England and Wales. With over 1,000 nature conservation areas, it is teeming with internationally important wildlife, including some of the rarest bird, mammal and insect life found anywhere in Europe.

During the summer months, the famous chalk grassland is bejewelled with an array of colourful wildflowers, which attract up to thirty different species of butterfly on the wing at any one time. Described as Europe's 'rainforest in miniature', the chalk grassland is a unique habitat that requires careful management by farmers and conservationists.

What makes this wildlife haven all the more special is its proximity to large urban areas. An hour from London and within easy reach of the south coast cities of Brighton, Portsmouth and Southampton, the South Downs offers an opportunity to escape urban life and the chance to breathe just a little more slowly.

The National Park is best known for the South Downs Way, one of sixteen National Trails in England and Wales. Running along the chalk escarpment, with stunning panoramic views at every turn, this 100-mile (160-km) route from Winchester to Eastbourne has been walked by humans for 5,000 years. Yet the South Downs Way is just one aspect of this walkers' paradise.

The South Downs is criss-crossed by an impressive network of rights of way, covering a total of 2,050 miles (3,300 km) and offering a chance to explore hidden hideaways and find your own slice of serenity.

Exercising in the sea air can be hungry and thirsty work, but with a tradition of inns and eateries, markets and farm shops, you are never far from local produce, mouth-watering fare and memorable foodie experiences.

A landscape rich in folklore and legend, it's little wonder that this picturesque area has provided inspiration for generations of writers, artists and storytellers, including the great Rudyard Kipling who was moved by 'Our blunt, bow-headed whale-backed Downs'.

Start your own South Downs journey and discover an area of inspirational beauty that promises to lift the soul.

Summer Solstice sunset celebrations at the Devil's Jumps Bronze Age barrows, Treyford.

Getting around

In the South Downs National Park you are never too far from a quaint village or market town.

Unlike many National Parks, which are virtually inaccessible without a car, the South Downs is an easy area to explore on public transport – or simply by walking or cycling out of the nearest town. This is perfect for those who want to go car-free, or for anyone wishing to visit one of the many pubs, breweries or vineyards along the way.

The area has a number of mainline railway stations that connect the south coast with London, the principal ones within the National Park being Petersfield and Lewes. The cathedral cities of Chichester and Winchester and seaside resorts such as Eastbourne and Brighton are great leaping-off points for access to the National Park.

The busy town of Farnham in Surrey is also a great base for discovering gems such as Alice Holt Forest.

The National Park's most popular beauty spots, attractions, cafés and pubs can get very busy on bank holiday weekends and during the Easter and summer school holidays, especially on sunny days. If crowds aren't your scene, head for one of the quieter areas. There are plenty of lesser-known treasures buried across the Downs – it doesn't take long to find them.

During the winter months, some museums and heritage attractions limit their opening hours, so remember to plan ahead.

Protecting the countryside

The South Downs National Park Authority wants everyone to enjoy their visit and to help keep the area a special place. You can do this by following the Countryside Code.
There are five sections of the code dedicated to helping members of the public respect, protect and enjoy the countryside.
These are:

- Be safe, plan ahead and follow any signs.
- Leave gates and property as you find them.
- Protect plants and animals and take your litter home.
- Keep dogs under close control, especially near farm animals and during the nesting season.
- Consider other people.

The National Park runs a 'Take The Lead' campaign, which encourages responsible dog walking and dogs to be kept on leads around livestock. Walkers should take extra care by sticking to paths during the bird nesting season between 1 March and 15 September.

Visit **www.southdowns.gov.uk** for more information.

Breathtaking views from Old Winchester Hill, which is also the site of an Iron Age hill fort.

Walking tips & guidance

Safety

As with all outdoor activities, walking is safe provided a few simple commonsense rules are followed:

- Make sure you are fit enough to complete the walk.
- Always try to let others know where you intend to go.
- Wear sensible clothes and suitable footwear.
- Take a map or guide.
- Always allow plenty of time for the walk and be aware of when it will get dark.
- Walk at a steady pace. A zigzag route is usually a more comfortable way of negotiating a slope. Avoid running directly downhill as it's easier to lose control and may also cause erosion to the hillside.
- When walking on country roads, walk on the right-hand side facing the oncoming traffic, unless approaching a blind bend ,when you should cross over to the left so as to be seen from both directions.
- Try not to dislodge stones on high edges or slopes.
- If the weather changes unexpectedly and visibility becomes poor, don't panic, but try to remember the last certain feature you passed and work out your route from that point on the map. Be sure of your route before continuing.

Unfortunately, accidents can happen even on easy walks. If you're with someone who has an accident or can't continue, you should:

- Make sure the injured person is sheltered from further injury, although you should never move anyone with a head, neck or back injury.

- If you have a phone with a signal, call for help.

- If you can't get a signal and have to leave the injured person to go for help, try to leave a note saying what has happened and what first aid you have tried. Make sure you know the exact location so you can give accurate directions to the emergency services. When you reach a telephone call 999 and ask for the police or mountain rescue.

Equipment

The equipment you will need depends on several factors, such as the type of activity planned, the time of year, and the weather likely to be encountered.

Clothing should be adequate for the day. In summer, remember sun screen, especially for your head and neck. Wear light woollen socks and lightweight boots or strong shoes. Even on hot days take an extra layer and waterproofs in your rucksack, just in case.

Winter wear is a much more serious affair. Remember that once the body starts to lose heat, it becomes much less efficient. Jeans are particularly unsuitable for winter walking.

When considering waterproof clothing, it pays to buy the best you can afford. Make sure that the jacket is loose-fitting, windproof and has a generous hood. Waterproof overtrousers will not only

offer protection against the rain, but they are also windproof. Clothing described as 'showerproof' will not keep you dry in heavy rain, and those made from rubberized or plastic materials can be heavy to carry and will trap moisture on the inside. Your rucksack should have wide, padded carrying straps for comfort.
It is important to wear boots that fit well or shoes with a good moulded sole – blisters can ruin any walk! Woollen socks are much more comfortable than any other fibre. Your clothes should be comfortable and not likely to catch on twigs and bushes.

It is important to carry a compass and a map or guide. A small first aid kit is also useful for treating cuts and other small injuries.

Finally, take a bottle of water and enough food to keep you going.

Public rights of way

Right of way means that anyone may walk freely on a defined footpath or ride a horse or bicycle along a public bridleway. In 1949, the National Parks and Access to the Countryside Act tidied up the law covering rights of way. Following public consultation, maps were drawn up by the Countryside Authorities of England and Wales to show all rights of way. Copies of these maps are available for public inspection and are invaluable when trying to resolve doubts over little-used footpaths. Once on the map, the right of way is irrefutable.

Any obstructions to a right of way should be reported to the local Highways Authority.

In England and Wales rights of way fall into three main categories:

- Public footpaths – for walkers only.
- Bridleways – for passage on foot, horseback or bicycle.
- Byways – for all the above and for motorized vehicles.

Free access to footpaths and bridleways does mean that certain guidelines should be followed as a courtesy to those who live and work in the area. For example, you should only sit down to picnic where it does not interfere with other walkers or the landowner. All gates must be kept closed to prevent stock from straying and dogs must be kept under close control – usually this is interpreted as meaning that they should be kept on a lead. Motorised vehicles must not be driven along a public footpath or bridleway without the landowner's consent.

A farmer may put a docile mature beef bull with a herd of cows or heifers, in a field crossed by a public footpath. Beef bulls such as Herefords (usually brown/red in colour) are unlikely to be upset by passers-by but dairy bulls, like the black-and-white Friesian, can be dangerous by nature. It is, therefore, illegal for a farmer to let a dairy bull roam loose in a field open to public access.

The Countryside and Rights of Way Act 2000 (the 'right to roam') allows access on foot to areas of legally defined 'open country' – mountain, moor, downland, heath and registered common land. It does not allow freedom to walk everywhere. It also increases protection for Sites of Special Scientific Interest, improves wildlife enforcement legislation and allows for better management of Areas of Outstanding Natural Beauty.

How to use this book

Each of the walks in this guide are set out in a similar way. They are all introduced with a simple locator map followed by a brief description of the area, its geography and history, and some notes on things you will encounter on your walk.

Near the start of each section there is a panel of information outlining the distance of the walk, the time it is expected to take and briefly describing the path conditions or the terrain you will encounter. A suggested starting point, along with grid reference is shown, as is the nearest postcode – although in rural locations postcodes can cover a large area and are therefore only a rough guide for sat nav users. It is always sensible to take a reference map with you, and the relevant OS Explorer map is also listed.

The major part of each section is taken up with a plan for each walk and detailed point by point, description of our recommended route, along with navigational tips and points of interest.

Here is a description of the main symbols on the route maps:

Motorway	Railway station	30m Contour height (m)
Trunk/primary road	Bus station/stop	Walk route
Secondary road	Car park	Optional route
Tertiary road	Castle	1 Route instruction
Residential/ unclassified road	Church	Open land
Service road	Lighthouse	Park/sports ground
Track	Interesting feature	Urban area
Pedestrian/ bridleway/cycleway	Tourist information	Woodland
Footway/path	Café	Nature reserve
Railway	Pub	Wetland
River/coast	Toilets	Lake

WALK 1

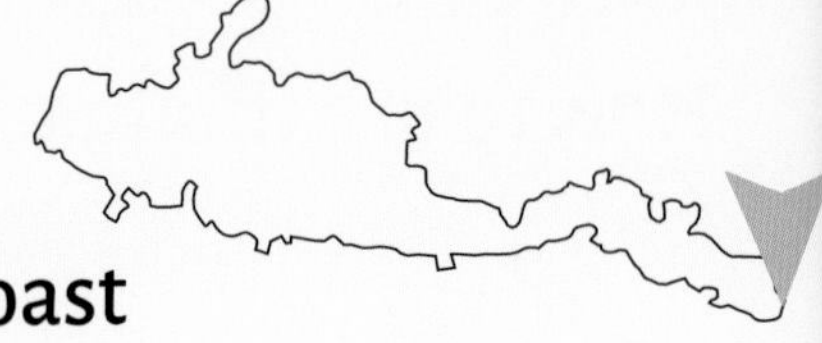

Sussex Heritage Coast

There's a magic to this coastline that can only be experienced by seeing the stunning landscape for yourself.

Featuring brilliant white cliffs backed by lush green downland, the Sussex coast between Eastbourne and Seaford was the first to be given Heritage Coast status. On sunny days, the landscape combines with turquoise seas to create a photographer's dream.

This walk, which has the option to be circular, starts on the west side of Eastbourne and takes you along a stretch of the coastal path, passing Beachy Head, the highest chalk sea cliff in Britain, with its picturesque lighthouse. Continuing along the clifftop, the route takes you past Belle Tout Lighthouse and Birling Gap, at the eastern end of the spectacular Seven Sisters cliffs, before turning back inland.

The cliffs along this coastline are receding at a rate of 30–40 cm each year, so remember to take notice of warning signs, as rock falls can happen at any time and there are overhangs and faults that you can't see from the path. Use your common sense and keep a safe distance from cliff edges and from the cliff face when on the beach.

Distance: 5 miles (8.1 km) (optional 2.1-mile (3.4 km) circle)
Time: 3½ hours (+ 50 mins for optional return section)
Terrain: Several gradual climbs.
Start: Near Eastbourne Golf Club (TV586986) (no parking at club)
Nearest Postcode: BN20 8ES
Map: OS Explorer OL25 Eastbourne & Beachy Head

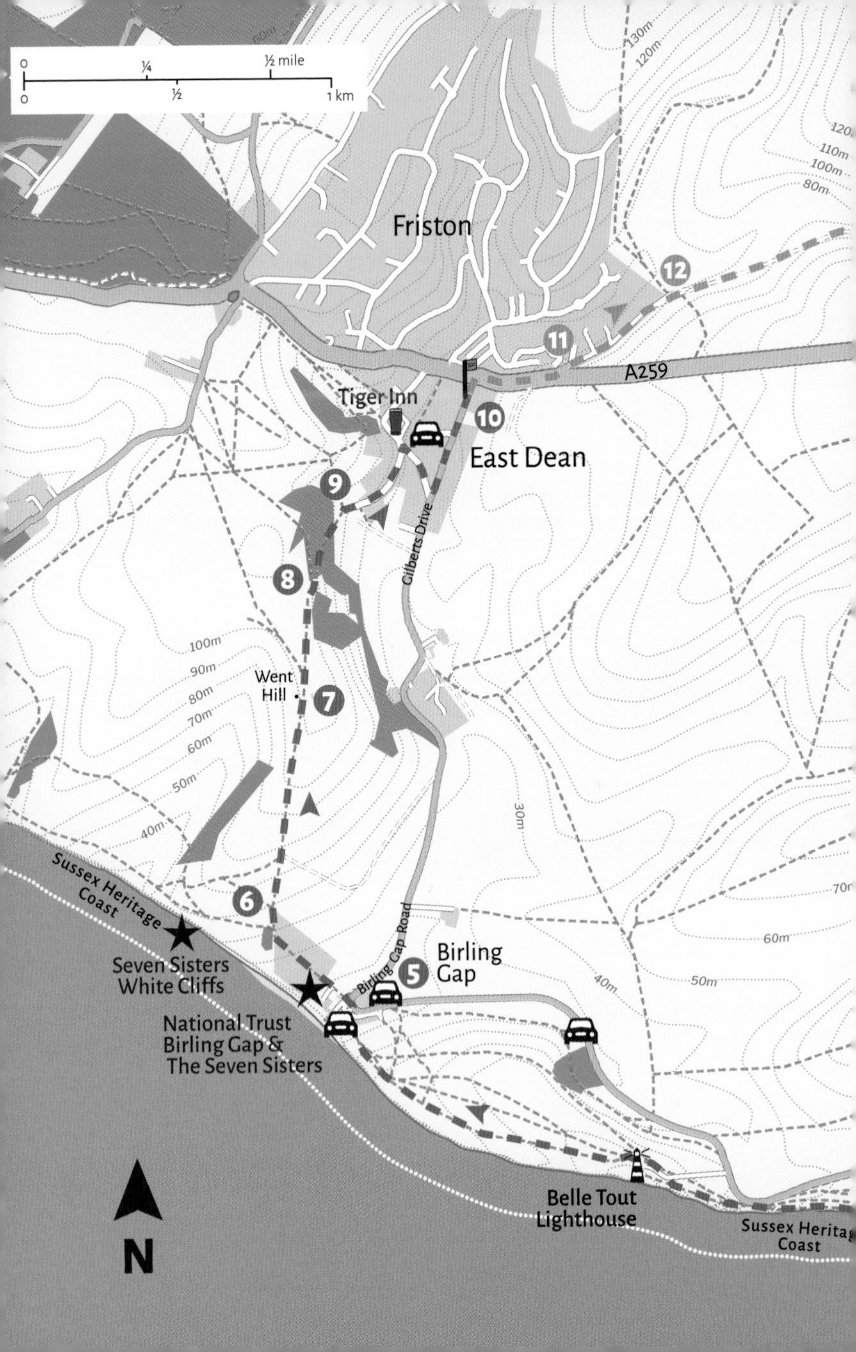

0
¼
½ mile
0
½
1 km
Friston
A259
Tiger Inn
East Dean
Gilberts Drive
Went Hill
100m
90m
80m
70m
60m
50m
40m
30m
Sussex Heritage Coast
Seven Sisters White Cliffs
National Trust Birling Gap & The Seven Sisters
Birling Gap Road
Birling Gap
Belle Tout Lighthouse
Sussex Heritag Coast
N

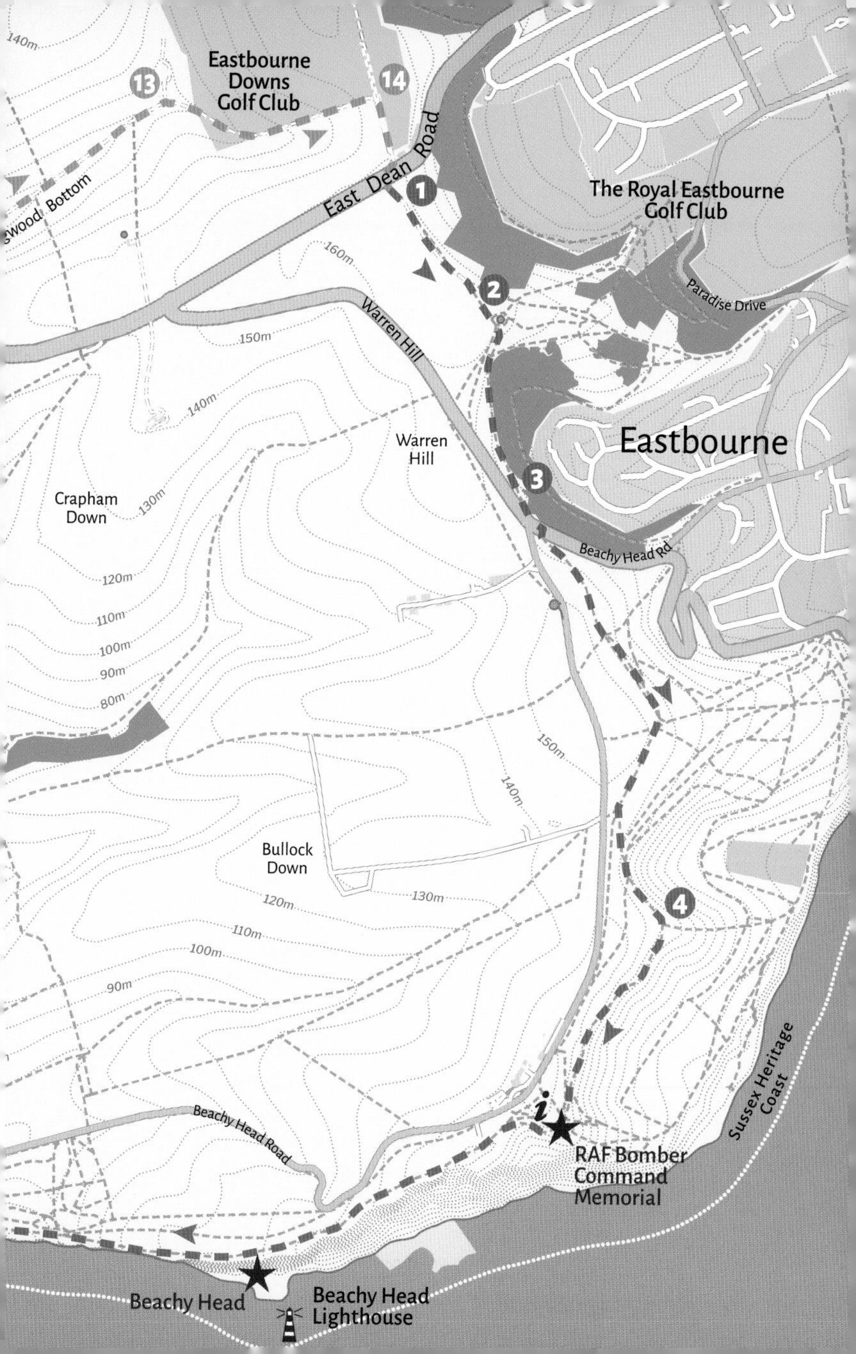

140m
Eastbourne Downs Golf Club
13
14
East Dean Road
1
swood Bottom
160m
The Royal Eastbourne Golf Club
2
Paradise Drive
Warren Hill
150m
140m
Warren Hill
Eastbourne
3
Crapham Down
130m
Beachy Head Rd
120m
110m
100m
90m
80m
150m
140m
Bullock Down
120m
130m
4
110m
100m
90m
Sussex Heritage Coast
Beachy Head Road
i
RAF Bomber Command Memorial
Beachy Head
Beachy Head Lighthouse

1. Starting opposite Eastbourne Downs golf course, on the seaward side of East Dean Road, take the sunken track towards the trig point, which comes into view as you walk along the path.

2. At the pond bear right of the trig point and, keeping on the Downs, follow the road to your right. Cross the road at the turning for Birling Gap, Beachy Head and the Countryside Centre.

3. Keep on the seaward side and follow the Downs over the brow of the hill.

4. With the sea on your left continue for about 3½ miles (5.5 km) to Birling Gap, via Beachy Head and Belle Tout lighthouse.

5. Immediately past the entrance to the car park at Birling Gap, take the chalk track up towards the houses on your left.

6. At the top of the track, go through the gap beside the gate and follow the blue bridleway sign up the hill, continuing in the direction you have just been walking.

7. Follow the path to the right of the red-tin-roofed barn. Keep the scrub on your right, and stay on the level.

8. Take the first path that drops down the side of the hill, on the right, and head straight on into East Dean, passing through a gate into the field and then a gate onto the access road for the houses.

9. Cross the village green, by the Tiger Inn, and turn right through the car park. Turn left onto the road out of the village and finish at the bus stop on the main road.

Optional return route

⑩ Cross the main road using the pedestrian crossing and turn right following the pavement uphill.

⑪ Turn left into Downs View Lane and follow the tarmac road ahead.

⑫ At the end of the road take the grassy track to the right of the metal farm gate. Passing a metal vehicle barrier follow the path for around 0.9 miles (1.5 km) through the dry valley of Ringwood Bottom.

⑬ After passing flint-walled fields on your left, bear right at Ringwood Farm to follow a concrete track uphill towards Eastbourne Downs Golf Club.

⑭ At the end of the concrete track, turn right and follow the South Downs Way blue bridleway signs to return to the A259 East Dean Road and your starting point.

WALK 2

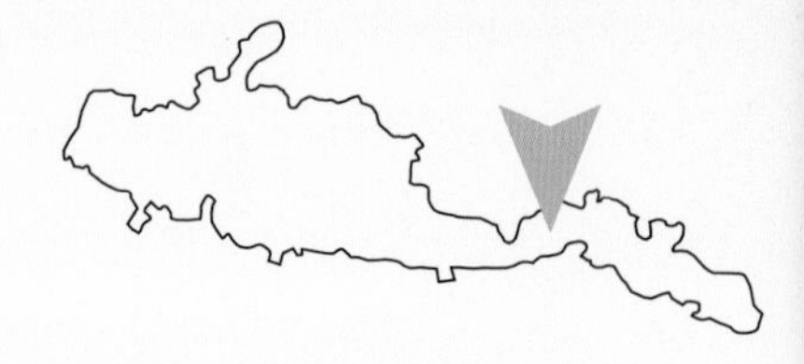

Devil's Dyke

This walk takes in stunning views of the English Channel and the unspoilt beauty of the Weald.

At nearly a mile long, the Dyke valley is the longest, deepest and widest 'dry valley' in the UK. Legend has it that the Devil dug this chasm in order to flood the churches and drown the parishioners of the Weald. Scientists, however, believe it was formed naturally, about 10,000 years ago when water from melting glaciers carved a valley into the chalkland at the end of the last ice age.

Venture into the valley during spring or summer and you will discover a living carpet of flowers – including several orchids, wild thyme, horseshoe vetch and bird's foot trefoil – and a myriad of colourful insects.

This circular walk takes in the ramparts of the Iron Age hillfort, which come into view as you walk around the hill. The remains of a ground-breaking Victorian theme park can also be seen a few minutes' walk from the car park.

The area is now managed and cared for by the National Trust.

Distance: 2½ miles (4 km)
Time: 1–1½ hours
Terrain: Some steep declines and moderate inclines, uneven in some places, with a loose surface. Gates.
Start/Finish: Devil's Dyke National Trust car park (TQ258110)
Nearest Postcode: BN1 8YJ
Map: OS Explorer OL11 Brighton & Hove

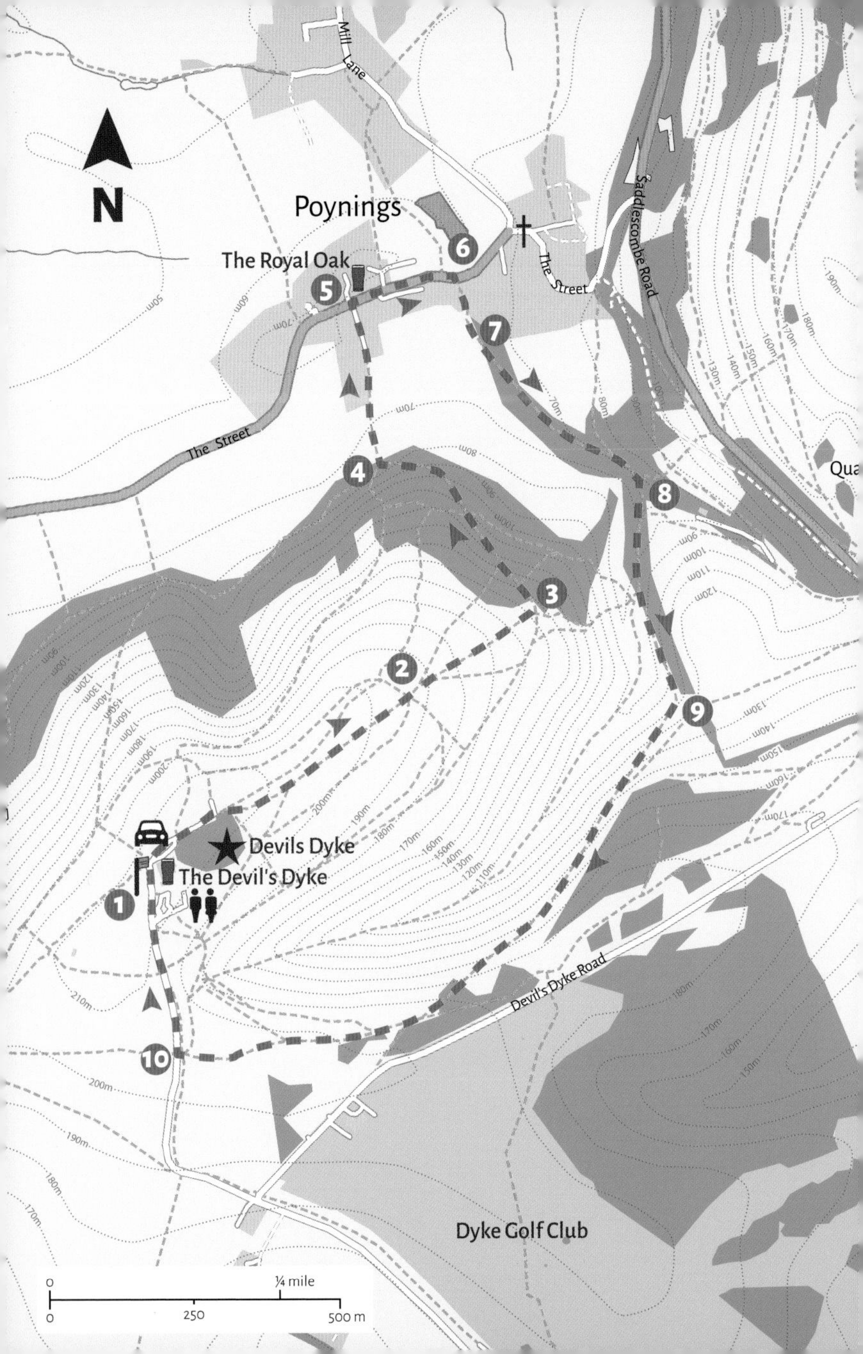

N
Poynings
Mill Lane
The Royal Oak
The Street
Saddlescombe Road
Devils Dyke
The Devil's Dyke
Devil's Dyke Road
Dyke Golf Club
1
2
3
4
5
6
7
8
9
10
0
¼ mile
0
250
500 m

1. Starting at the bus stop just before the National Trust car park, head up past the Devil's Dyke pub (on your right). Follow the signposts across the car park, passing through a metal barrier. Continue straight along the marked footpath.

2. Go straight ahead at the crossroads of paths, over the stile and down the hill, turning left onto the bridleway.

3. Continue along the bridleway through the wood. Take care on the steep track, as this can be slippery when wet.

4. At the bottom of the steep track turn right past the gardens.

5. At the road turn right and head into Poynings.

6. Continue to the Royal Oak pub, then at the period garage turn right, keeping the small stream on your left, and head through the gate.

7. At the next gate turn left and cross the waterway. Continue along the path into the wood, keeping the water on your right.

8. Continue to the gate which leads to an open area and into the valley bottom of Devil's Dyke. For the best views follow the bridleway which leads up to the left side of Devil's Dyke.

9. At the top of the slope the bridleway joins the South Downs Way. Turn right here and continue to the road.

10. Turn right and follow the path alongside the road to return to the bus stop.

The landscape painter John Constable described the panorama from Devil's Dyke as 'the grandest view in the world'.

WALK 3

Liphook and Milland

This walk is popular with visitors looking to escape the big city as Liphook is so accessible.

This lovely circular walk provides the opportunity to discover rolling fields and the remnants of Britain's great iron-making era. Like much of the Sussex Weald, the area between Liphook and Milland was once the location of a prosperous iron industry, evidence of which can still be seen around the privately owned Milland House and Milland Place.

The stream that flows from Milland Place through the former mill is called Hammer Stream, a name reflecting the industrial heritage of the area: a 'hammer' was a pond created to drive water-powered forges and iron furnaces.

Hammer Stream flows into the millpond of the early eighteenth century mill, a three-storey building where the disused iron wheel can still be seen.

Starting from Liphook railway station on the main Waterloo line, this walk is within easy reach of London.

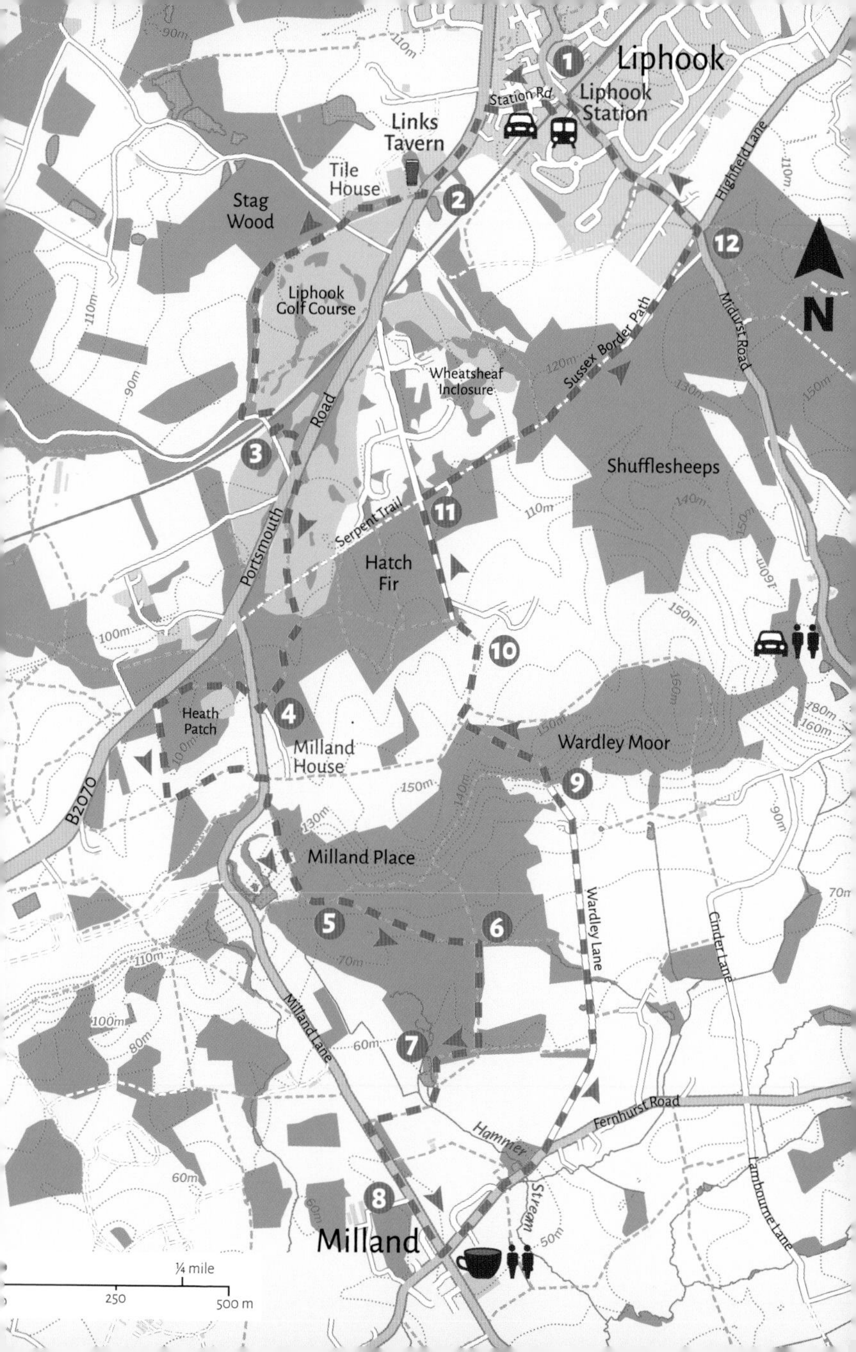

Liphook
Liphook Station
Station Rd
Links Tavern
Tile House
Stag Wood
Liphook Golf Course
Wheatsheaf Inclosure
Sussex Border Path
Highfield Lane
Midhurst Road
Shufflesheeps
Serpent Trail
Portsmouth Road
Hatch Fir
Heath Patch
Milland House
Wardley Moor
B2070
Milland Place
Wardley Lane
Cinder Lane
Milland Lane
Fernhurst Road
Hammer Stream
Lambourne Lane
Milland
N
¼ mile
250
500 m
1
2
3
4
5
6
7
8
9
10
11
12

Distance: 7¼ miles (11.5 km)
Time: 3–4 hours
Terrain: One steep climb of 125 ft (45 m) at Wardley Hanger. Forested paths (can be muddy) with stiles, and public roads.
Start/Finish: Liphook Railway Station (SU841309)
Nearest Postcode: GU30 7DN
Map: OS Explorer OL33 Haslemere & Petersfield

❶ Turn left out of Liphook railway station, then left onto Station Road. At the T-junction turn left towards Portsmouth and Petersfield.

❷ At the Links Tavern, cross the main road and follow the bridleway bearing to the right of the road. Continue past Tile House, cross the lane and follow the bridleway along the right-hand edge of Liphook Golf Course. Follow bridleway signs straight ahead until you reach a road; turn left.

❸ Cross the railway bridge and follow the road past the fifth golf tee. Cross the main road again and take the bridleway directly opposite which immediately bends to the right. Pass the practice driving range on your right and cross the broad track of the Serpent Trail. Continue ahead on the narrower bridleway through the woods. At the end of the golf course turn right at the T-junction onto the track which bears right and descends to a road.

❹ Turn right at the road; left at the first bridleway sign and then bear left at the next junction. Take the next left and follow the power lines. Where the power lines bear left, continue straight on to the fence line; keeping the fence on your left join the footpath following the fence round. Half way along, cross into the field following the signpost and aim straight ahead for Milland House. Turn right at the road and walk along the verge for a short distance. Cross the road and take the bridleway track on the other side.

❺ Follow the path for a short distance, round a bend to the left, and then at a fork in the path, bear right heading downhill.

❻ Turn right at the junction of paths. At the T-junction turn right and almost immediately bear left through trees into a field.

❼ Cross the field to a gate. Pass the old mill on your right and continue to a wooden footbridge. Follow the gravel track straight ahead to the road and turn left into Milland.

❽ After passing Jubilee Beacon at Cartersland Green on your right (originally lit for the Queen's Diamond Jubilee in 2012), continue to the crossroads. If you fancy some refreshments at this point nip straight over the crossroads to the Milland Community Shop and Café or continue the walk by turning left at the crossroads towards Linch. After Durrants Pond, turn left along Wardley Lane and continue until the tarmac ends (just beyond Robins Cottage).

❾ Take the right-hand branch where the track forks to climb Wardley Hanger. At the top of the hill continue straight ahead on the bridleway.

❿ After 200 m, at a junction of paths, take the footpath left and downhill. Join the driveway of Hatch House and continue straight ahead on the drive.

⓫ After a quarter of a mile (400 m), at the crossroads of paths, turn right onto the restricted byway, following the Serpent Trail. Continue through woodland with the extensive gardens of the Wheatsheaf enclosure on your left.

⓬ Continue for 0.6 miles (1 km) and fork left on a byway to the main road. Turn left, keeping to the footpath and cross the railway footbridge. Turn right down the steps to return to the station.

WALK 4

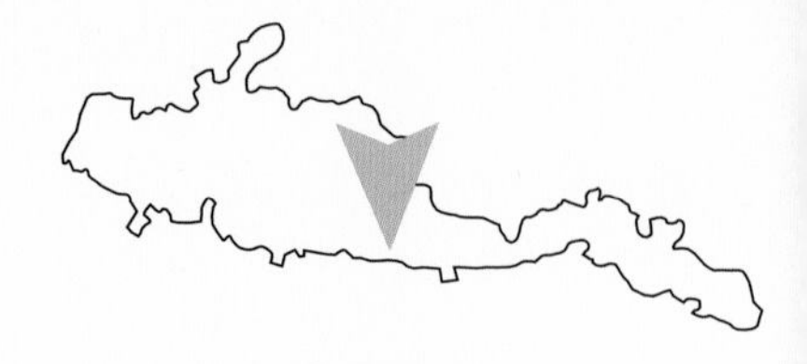

Arundel

This is a gentle walk in stunning surroundings that is perfect for a summer's day.

The majestic castle at Arundel has a thousand years of history, which is told through the surviving Norman keep and gatehouse, the restorations made after it was damaged during the Civil War, and the extensive nineteenth-century remodelling. The second-largest castle in England, it has been the seat of the Dukes of Norfolk for over 700 years, and sits high on a hill overlooking the River Arun as it meanders down the valley and through the town of Arundel.

This walk takes you through the eastern end of the historic market town, past the castle and on towards the WWT Arundel Wetland Centre, a 65-acre nature reserve on the banks of the river. You have the option to extend the walk here by taking the path around the beautiful Swanbourne Lake. Starting life as a millpond, Swanbourne Lake has records dating back to the Domesday Book in the 11th century. In the late 18th century, during work to Arundel Park, the pond was enlarged to form the current lake which is fed mainly by groundwater springs known as the 'Blue Springs' due to the colour of the water as it comes out of the ground.

From here, a riverside path brings you back to the town. The area provides a valuable habitat for an array of wildlife, so look out for wildfowl, water voles and kingfishers as you go.

Distance: 3½ miles (5.6 km) (optional 2-mile (3.2-km) loop around Swanbourne Lake)
Time: 1½–2 hours (+ 1 hour for optional loop)
Terrain: Fairly flat with some small inclines. Grassy paths, uneven in places.
Start/Finish: Arundel Station (TQ023063)
Nearest Postcode: BN18 9PH
Map: OS Explorer OL10 Arundel & Pulborough

❶ Starting in front of Arundel railway station, follow the shared-use path to the right which passes underneath the road. Proceed into Arundel.

❷ Cross Arundel Bridge, which takes you over the River Arun, and turn right onto Mill Road.

❸ Continue straight along Mill Road looking out for water voles, which thrive in the waterway alongside the road.

❹ When the Mill Road footway runs out by the entrance to the old dairy (now a private residence), carefully cross the road. If you wish to return from this point to Arundel along the river, turn right immediately before Swanbourne footbridge, and follow the path alongside the Millstream. Follow the remaining directions from point 7.

❺ To continue to Arundel Wetland Centre or to take the optional route around Swanbourne Lake, cross the Millstream using the footbridge. Head down the steps then back up to re-join the road. For a short distance there is no footpath (between the bridge and the Swanbourne Lodge tea rooms at the entrance to Swanbourne Lake), but the road is wide and visibility is good. If you'd like to visit the Arundel Wetland Centre, continue with care along Mill Road for an additional 200 m. For those wishing to explore Swanbourne Lake, follow the footpath around the lake which brings you out close to Swanbourne footbridge.

❻ To continue with the river walk, head down the steps from the road to Swanbourne footbridge and take the footpath on your left immediately after the bridge. This footpath runs alongside the Millstream up to where it meets the River Arun.

❼ Turn right and follow the footpath beside the River Arun as it bends slowly back into Arundel and re-trace your steps to the railway station.

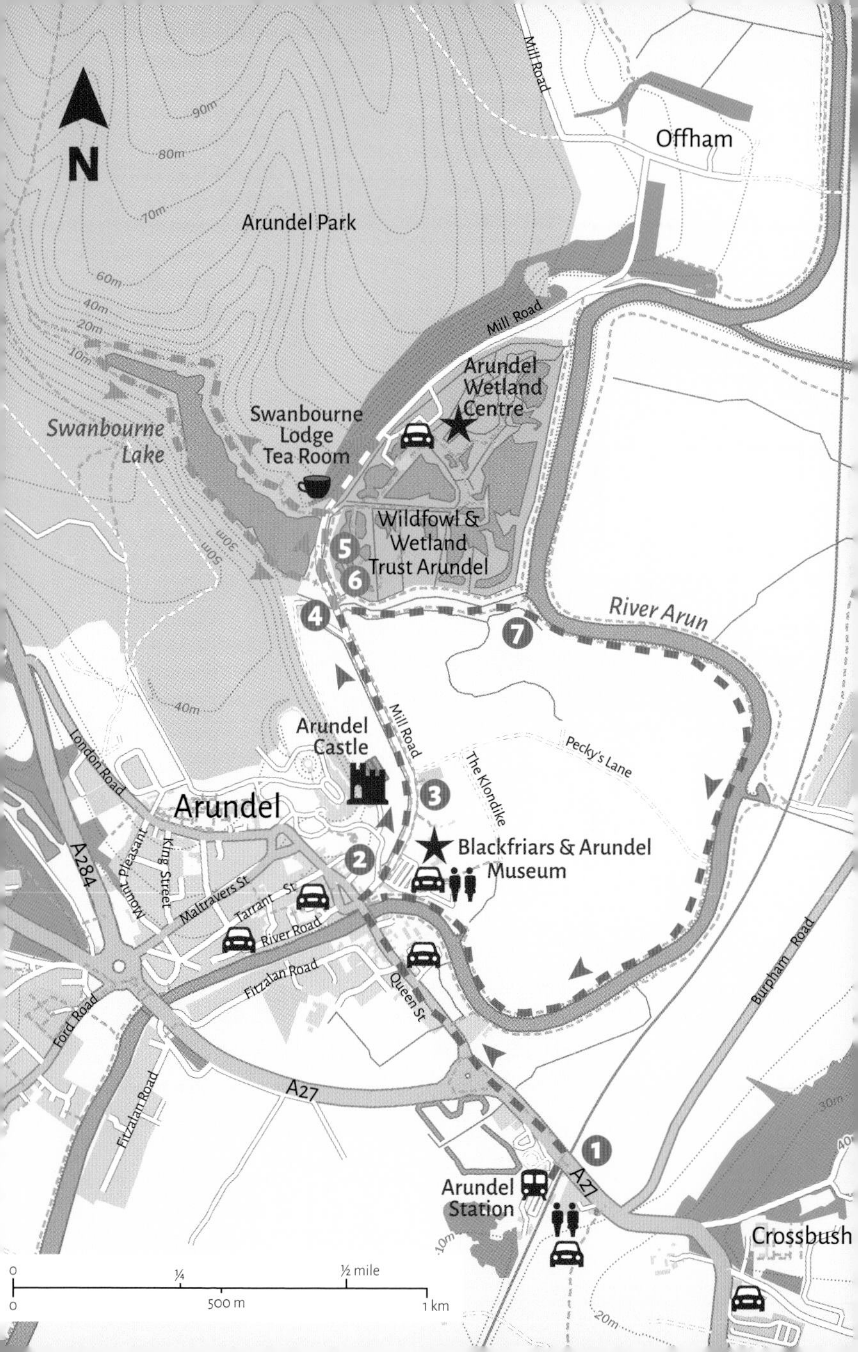
N
Offham
Mill Road
Arundel Park
90m
80m
70m
60m
40m
20m
10m
Mill Road
Arundel Wetland Centre
Swanbourne Lodge Tea Room
Swanbourne Lake
Wildfowl & Wetland Trust Arundel
30m
50m
River Arun
40m
Mill Road
Arundel Castle
Pecky's Lane
The Klondike
London Road
Arundel
Blackfriars & Arundel Museum
A284
Mount Pleasant
King Street
Maltravers St
Tarrant St
River Road
Fitzalan Road
Queen St
Burpham Road
Ford Road
Fitzalan Road
A27
A27
Arundel Station
30m
40
10m
Crossbush
20m
0
¼
½ mile
0
500 m
1 km

WALK 5

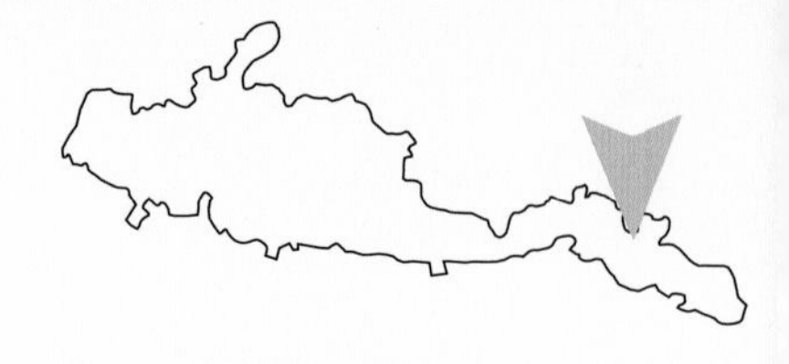

Hamsey

The views on this pleasant walk sum up the diversity of the landscape.

The East Sussex village of Hamsey gives its name to a parish that also includes the villages of Cooksbridge and Offham. Here you can discover a variety of landscapes, ranging from high chalk downland, the water meadows of the River Ouse and the heavy clay pasture and woodlands of the Low Weald.

Clues to this area's industrial past can be seen at the chalk pit on Offham Hill, where the extraction of chalk during the eighteenth and nineteenth centuries has shaped the local landscape. The proximity of the historic river highway to the chalk of the Downs provided the perfect opportunity to exploit this raw material. After being loosened by gunpowder, the chalk was dug away before being heated in on-site kilns to create lime. The lime was then transported by river barges to farms in the Weald where it was used to fertilise the wheat fields.

Enjoy a walk through the area's industrial heritage on this circular route through the three villages, past the chalk pit and along the bank of the River Ouse.

Distance: 3 miles (4.8 km)
Time: 2 hours
Terrain: Footpaths and bridleways with some pavements.
Start/Finish: Cooksbridge Station (TQ400135)
Nearest Postcode: BN8 4SW
Map: OS Explorer OL11 Brighton & Hove

❶ Exit Cooksbridge railway station from the northbound platform and cross the road.

❷ Take the tarmac path between the picket fence; follow it round past a playground, then left down a footpath running alongside the stream.

❸ Cross the footbridge, head towards a stile and carefully cross the railway track (stop and look both ways before crossing). Turn right at the fingerpost and follow the fence line on your right.

❹ At the next fingerpost turn left alongside the hedge.

❺ At the opening in the hedge follow the footpath waymarker diagonally across the field towards the furthest corner.

❻ Exit the field opposite Hamsey Manor and turn right on the road.

❼ Turn left down Whitfeld Lane and continue to Ivors Lane.

❽ At the junction take the track in front of you signposted 'Sussex Ouse Valley Way'.

❾ Go through the kissing gate, passing a pillbox on your right, and follow the embankment.

❿ Turn right to pass under the railway, following the path with the chalk pit cut on your left.

⓫ Go through the gate and turn right along the Old Coach Road.

⓬ At the road, turn left and head towards the church until you reach the main road (A275) opposite the Blacksmiths Arms pub.

⓭ Turn right and follow the pavement which runs alongside the road back to Cooksbridge Station.

0
¼ mile
0
250
500 m
N
Beechwood Lane
Cooksbridge Station
Cooksbridge
Hamsey Lane
North End Lane
Hamsey
Whitfeld Lane
The Drove
B2116
A275
Offham
Ivors Lane
Blacksmiths Arms
Pillbox
River Ouse
Old Coach Road
Chalkpit Cut
Papermill Cut
Landport Farm Rd
Churchill Rd
Pellbrook Rd
Landport Rd
Crisp Rd
Blois Road
Evelyn Rd
Eridge Green
Race Hill
Highdown Rd
Nevill Road
Offam Road
Lewes
Monks Way
Old Malling Way
Church Lane
1
2
3
4
5
6
7
8
9
10
11
12
13

The countryside around the village of Hamsey is a patchwork of lush green fields, downs and woodlands.

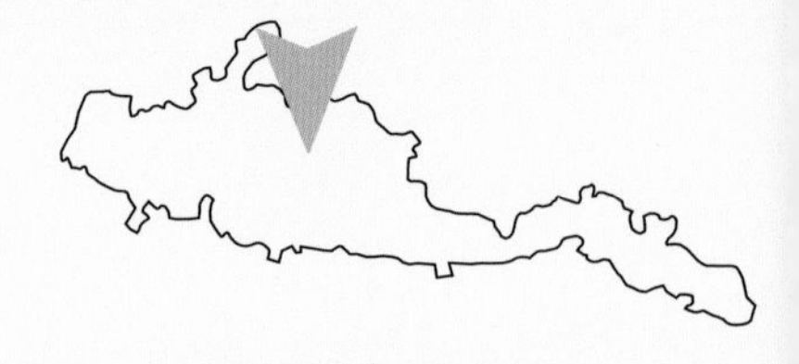

WALK 6
Midhurst

Midhurst is at the heart of the South Downs National Park and offers a wonderful mix of history, culture and picturesque views.

The magnificent Cowdray Ruins dominate the water meadows in the thriving market town of Midhurst. Their enduring presence today, thanks to restoration following a devastating fire in 1793, provides an insight into life during Tudor times, when the house was visited by Henry VIII and Elizabeth I.

During the 1880s, author H. G. Wells resided in the house beside the Angel Hotel and some of his early novels are based in the Midhurst area. Today, the distinctive yellow window frames seen on some buildings is the signature colour of the Cowdray Estate.

If enjoying this lovely circular walk during spring, look out for the flowers of pink purslane and river water crowfoot along the River Rother. You may also be lucky to spot the quick flash of a kingfisher or a bobbing grey wagtail along fast-flowing stretches. During the summer months the beautiful metallic-blue banded demoiselles, a type of damselfly, gather in large numbers by the river.

Midhurst is home to the South Downs Centre, a visitor centre and hub for the South Downs National Park. Discover more about the history of the South Downs and its incredible biodiversity by immersing yourself in the colourful exhibition displays.

Distance: 1.1 miles (1.7 km)
Time: ½–1 hour
Terrain: Uneven ground, muddy in places, steep ascent to St Ann's Hill.
Start/Finish: Midhurst South Downs Centre (SU886217)
Nearest Postcode: GU29 9DH
Map: OS Explorer OL33 Haslemere & Petersfield

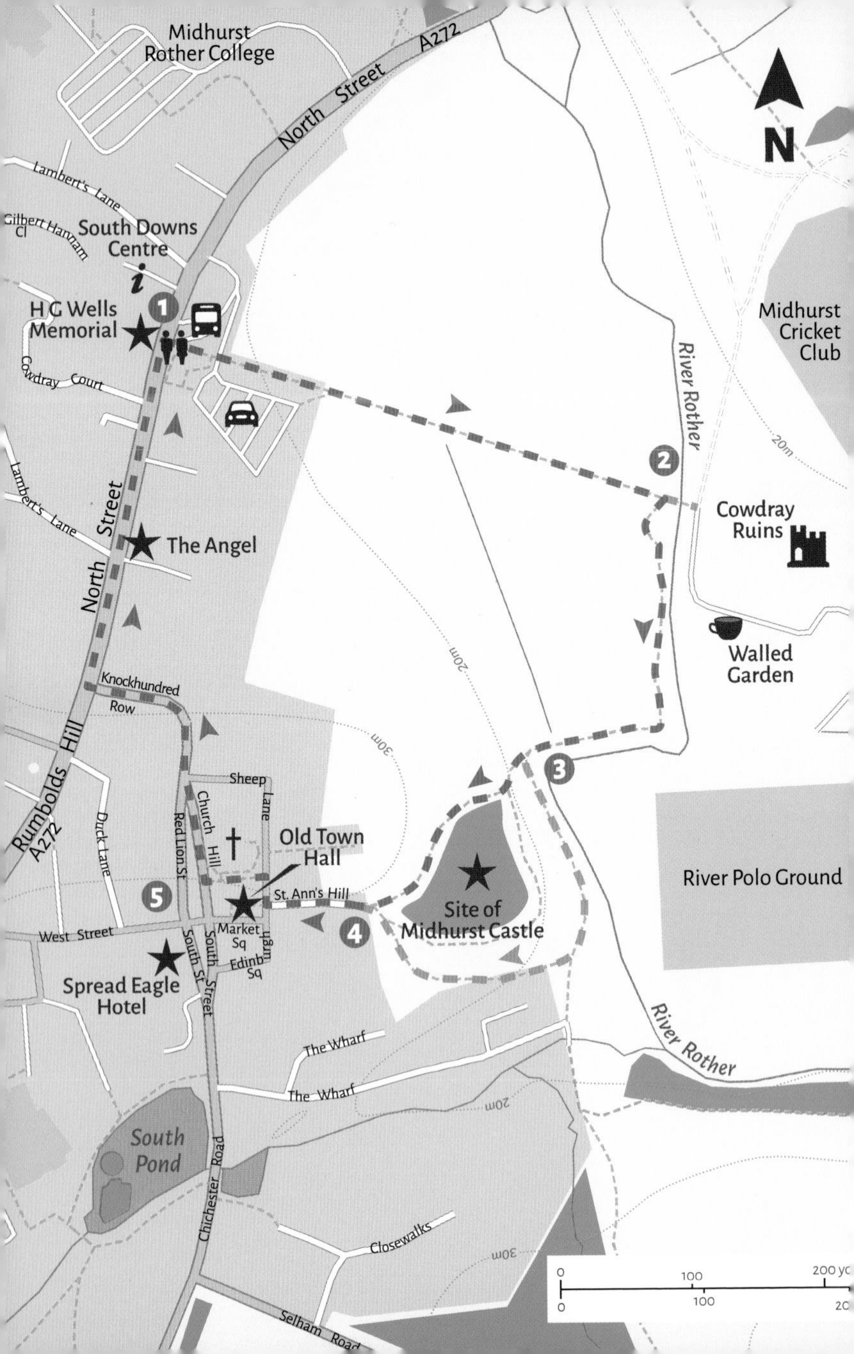
Midhurst Rother College
A272
North Street
N
Lambert's Lane
Gilbert Hannam Cl
South Downs Centre
i
1
H G Wells Memorial
Cowdray Court
Midhurst Cricket Club
River Rother
2
20m
Cowdray Ruins
Lambert's Lane
North Street
The Angel
Walled Garden
20m
Knockhundred Row
30m
3
Rumbolds Hill
A272
Sheep Lane
Church Hill
Red Lion St
Duck Lane
Old Town Hall
River Polo Ground
5
St. Ann's Hill
Site of Midhurst Castle
4
West Street
Market Sq
Edinb Sq
Spread Eagle Hotel
South St
South Street
River Rother
The Wharf
The Wharf
20m
South Pond
Chichester Road
Closewalks
30m
Selham Road
0
100
200 yd
0
100

❶ From the bus stop near to the North Street car park head through the gate towards the Cowdray Ruins across the causeway. Make a short detour here to take in the ruins or to visit the beautiful Walled Garden (free) and café.

❷ Just before you get to the river bridge turn right and follow the field edge with the river on your left until you get to a kissing gate (Note: cattle are sometimes grazing here).

❸ Enter the woodland and either climb the steps straight ahead, or continue to the left along the river until you reach an open area and follow the path uphill to the right. Either route will bring you to St Ann's Hill where, if you look carefully, you will find the remains of an Iron Age fort and a Norman castle. Modern-day Midhurst developed around this site.

❹ Below the remains, go through the gate and down a side street, called St Ann's Hill, into the market square where you can still see the old stocks. There are many historic buildings to admire nearby including the church – originally part of the castle – and the Spread Eagle Hotel, one of England's oldest coaching inns.

❺ Turn right and follow the pavement around past the old Town Hall, then go right, along Church Hill and round to Knockhundred Row. This brings you to the high street, where you turn right to return to the start.

WALK 7
River Itchen

The crystal-clear waters of the River Itchen create a place of tranquillity and reflection for walkers.

Flowing through the western South Downs, the River Itchen is prized for the clarity of its water, which is filtered through the porous chalk of the surrounding area. It is believed to have provided inspiration for Charles Kingsley's classic children's novel *The Water Babies*. The river flows through the village of Itchen Abbas, which was visited regularly by the author during Victorian times.

Charles Kingsley, a clergyman, intended his book to be a comment in support of Charles Darwin's theory of evolution, which had been published just a few years earlier. Today, it is easy to see how the environment around the river could inspire an interest in nature. The clear waters of the river provide an excellent habitat for freshwater species, including the rare white-clawed crayfish, and the banks play host to a variety of insects, birds and mammals such as badgers and otters.

This walk starts in Itchen Abbas and takes a figure-of-eight route, crossing the river four times and passing through a handful of small Hampshire villages along the way.

Distance: 4 miles (6.4 km)
Time: 2 hours
Terrain: Mainly level. Loose surface, can be muddy. River footbridges may be slippery.
Start/Finish: Itchen Abbas car park (SU535329)
Nearest Postcode: SO21 1BQ
Map: OS Explorer OL32 Winchester

1 From Itchen Abbas, pass the little church and cross the rivers by the road bridges on Avington Lane. Turn right at the T-junction, towards Avington.

2 Follow the road through the village, then turn right into Avington Park, enjoying views of the mansion at the lakeside.

3 Leave the park by the road and take the next footpath right at the edge of the wood to cross the river to Chilland.

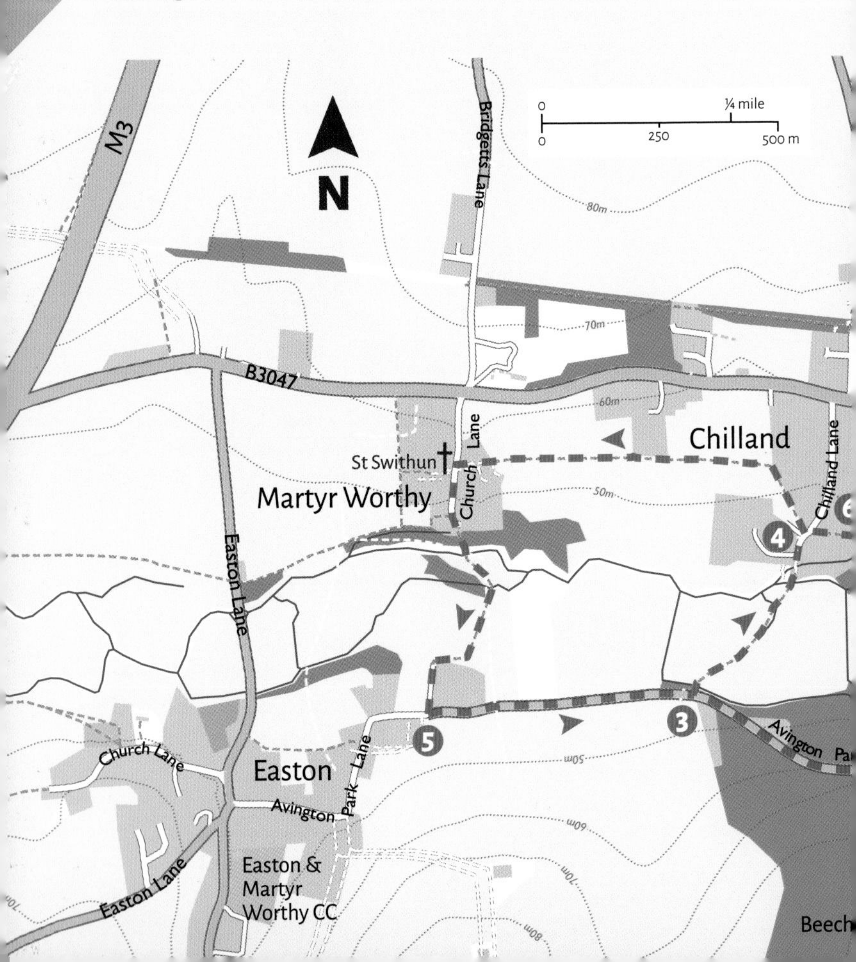

❹ A few steps up the road, turn left and head west along a footpath towards Martyr Worthy church. Here, turn left and cross the river by footbridges to reach the village of Easton.

❺ Turn left at the road, then left again to cross back over the river towards Chilland.

❻ Now turn right along a footpath running beside a tall brick wall. This path eventually opens out at a lovely spot on the river where the path forks in two. Follow the right fork back to Itchen Abbas.

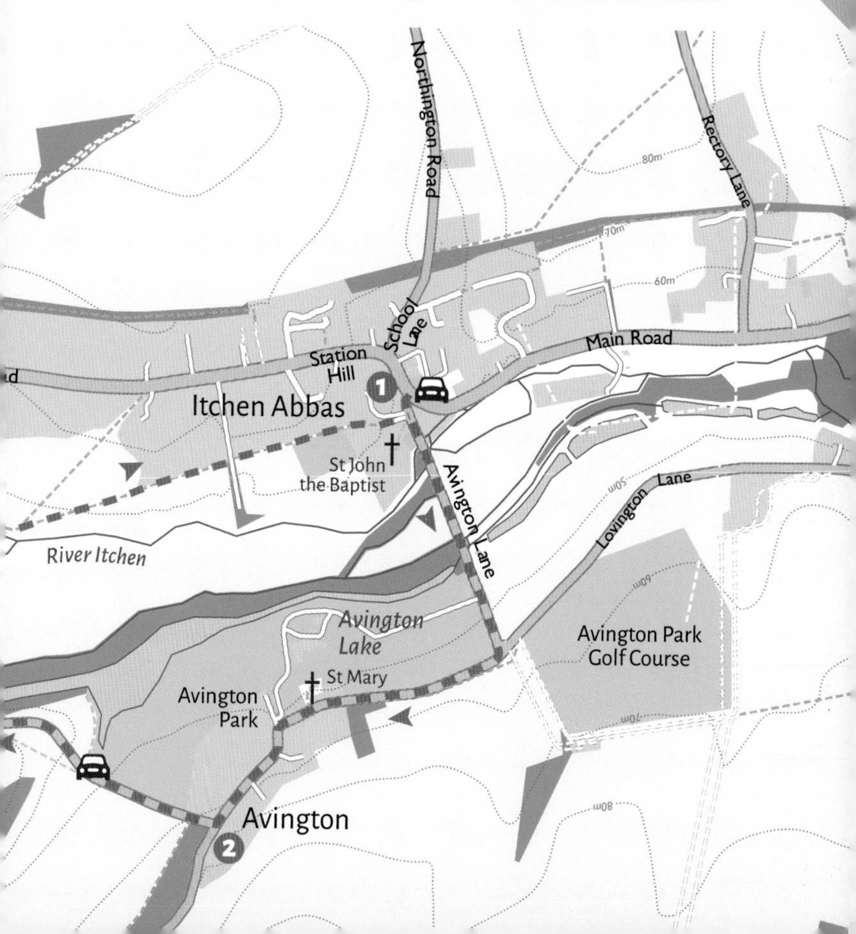

The River Itchen provides the perfect setting for a summer's evening spent watching for wildlife.

WALK 8

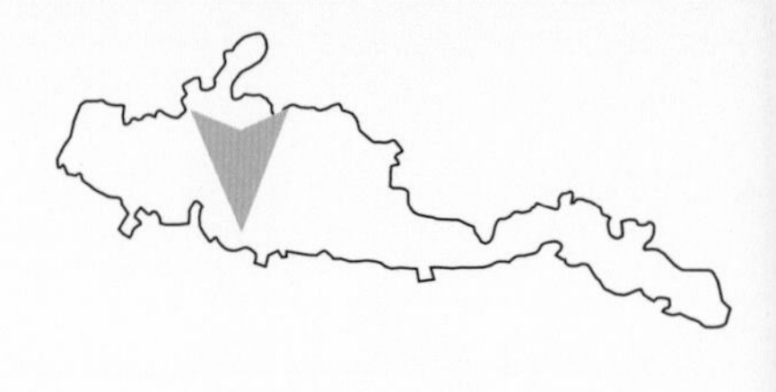

Stoughton to Kingley Vale

Kingley Vale has to be one of the most enchanting natural spaces in Europe.

There's a magic about Kingley Vale. The reserve contains one of the finest yew forests in western Europe, including a grove of ancient trees that are among the oldest living things in Britain.

Kingley Vale also has superb chalk grassland, which supports an abundance of wildlife including green woodpeckers, buzzards, red kites and butterflies galore.

This circular walk includes a steep climb that is rewarded with spectacular views of the South Coast and the spire of Chichester Cathedral. The route takes you past several interesting features including the Devil's Humps Bronze Age burial site – one of fourteen scheduled ancient monuments in the area – as well as the Tansley Stone, which commemorates the naturalist Sir Arthur Tansley, one of the founders of the reserve.

Distance: 4 miles (6.4 km)
Time: 1½ hours
Terrain: A steep ascent to top of Downs. No stiles or gates.
Start/Finish: Stoughton car park (SU801114)
Nearest Postcode: PO18 9JL
Map: OS Explorer OL8 Chichester

❶ Starting at the noticeboard at the centre of Stoughton, opposite the post box in the wall, follow the lane south in the direction of Racton. After 165 metres turn left at the bridleway fingerpost. Carry on past the memorial to the Polish pilot.

❷ Continue up the steep hill to the end of the wood, with Lord Mountbatten's polo field on your right. After 50 metres turn left onto the bridleway that takes you through mixed woodland at the edge of Kingley Vale forest and on to open grassland and the Devil's Humps. Tansley Stone is just beyond this, away from the path to the right.

❸ Continue along the bridleway through the woods. After a gradual descent of 1¼ miles (2 km), the woods give way to open fields to the left.

❹ At 5-bridleways fingerpost turn left onto 'Monarch's Way'. Follow the valley path downhill towards the distant cattle sheds. Once you have passed these to your left, carry on towards more sheds directly in front of you. Bear right towards the lane.

❺ Turn left onto the lane towards the Hare & Hounds pub and back to the start.

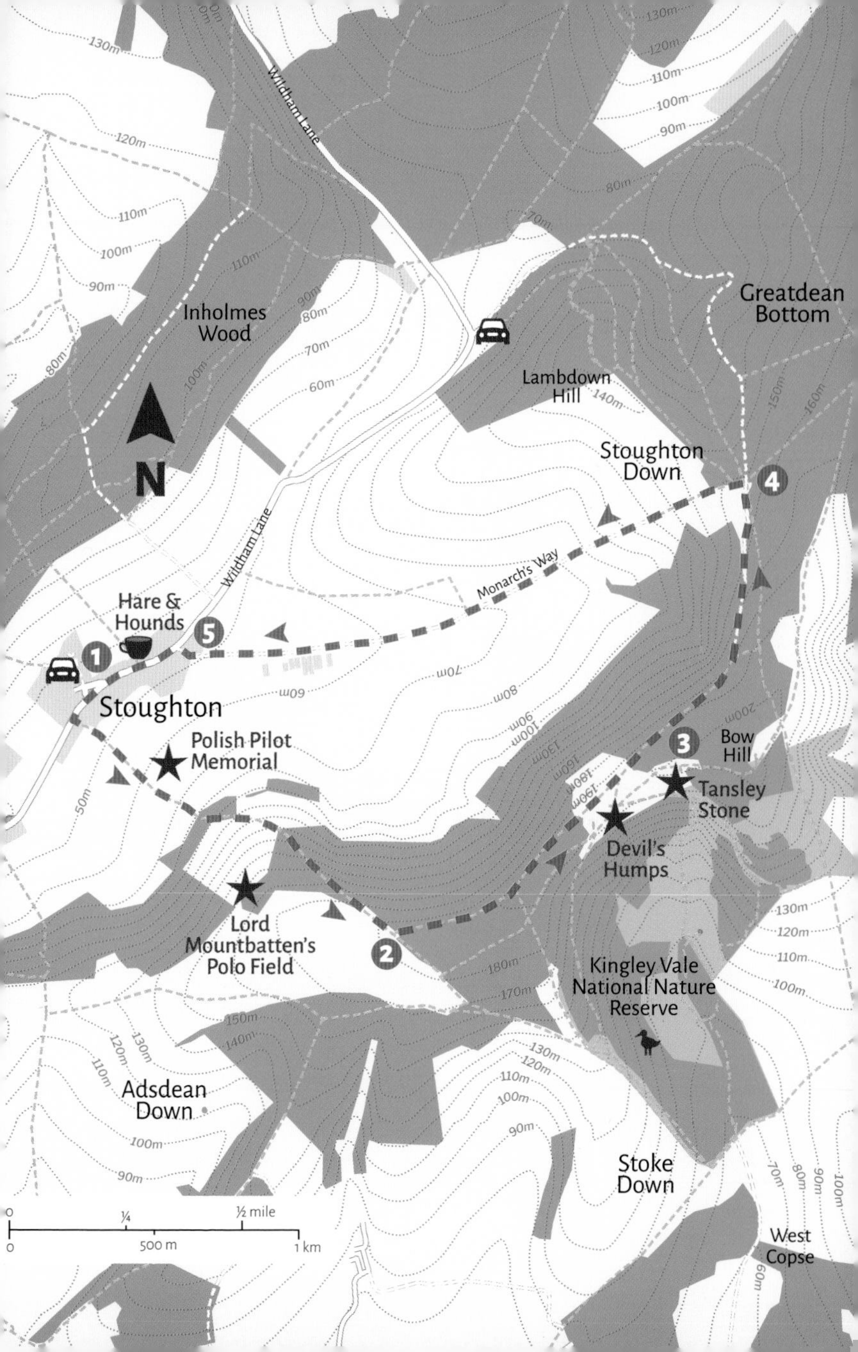

Wildham Lane
Inholmes Wood
Greatdean Bottom
Lambdown Hill
Stoughton Down
Monarch's Way
Hare & Hounds
Stoughton
Polish Pilot Memorial
Bow Hill
Tansley Stone
Devil's Humps
Lord Mountbatten's Polo Field
Kingley Vale National Nature Reserve
Adsdean Down
Stoke Down
West Copse
N
1
2
3
4
5
0
¼
½ mile
500 m
1 km

This dew pond at Kingley Vale is typical of many across the South Downs. Traditionally used for watering livestock, they now make a valuable habitat for wildlife.

WALK 9

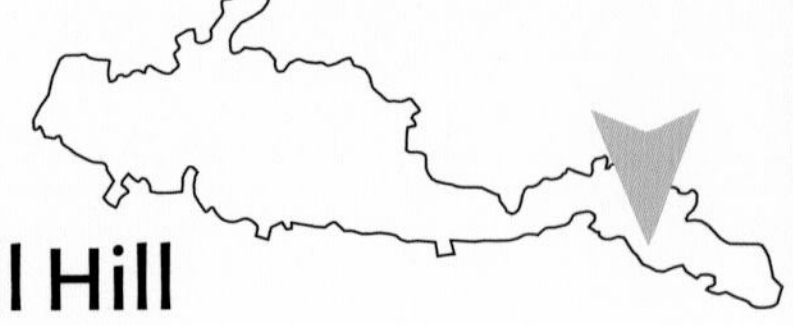

Telscombe and Mill Hill

A shimmering dew pond with dancing dragonflies is a magnificent sight for any walker.

It's worth taking time out to explore the picturesque village of Telscombe. The village has retained its peaceful character thanks to the wealthy bookmaker Ambrose Gorham who left the village to a trust known as 'Gorham's Gift'.

Dew ponds are a charming highlight of this walk. The porous chalk of the South Downs means there are few natural ponds, streams or rivers in the area. Dew ponds, of which Telscombe and Rodmell are good examples, were created to provide watering places for livestock. The ponds' saucer-like shape and clay lining allowed them to catch and retain water.

Many restored dew ponds are now wildlife havens, and are fenced to prevent livestock from getting in. They attract dragonflies and other insects, amphibians and birds. In the summer, watch out for swallows swooping down to catch flies and to take a drink.

This circular walk takes you from the village of Telscombe to the summit of Mill Hill, where you can enjoy views of the surrounding countryside.

Distance: 5½ miles (8.8 km)
Time: 2 hours
Terrain: Slight inclines, two steep sections.
Start/Finish: Bus stop on Telscombe Road (TQ408026)
Nearest Postcode: BN10 7UB
Map: OS Explorer OL11 Brighton & Hove

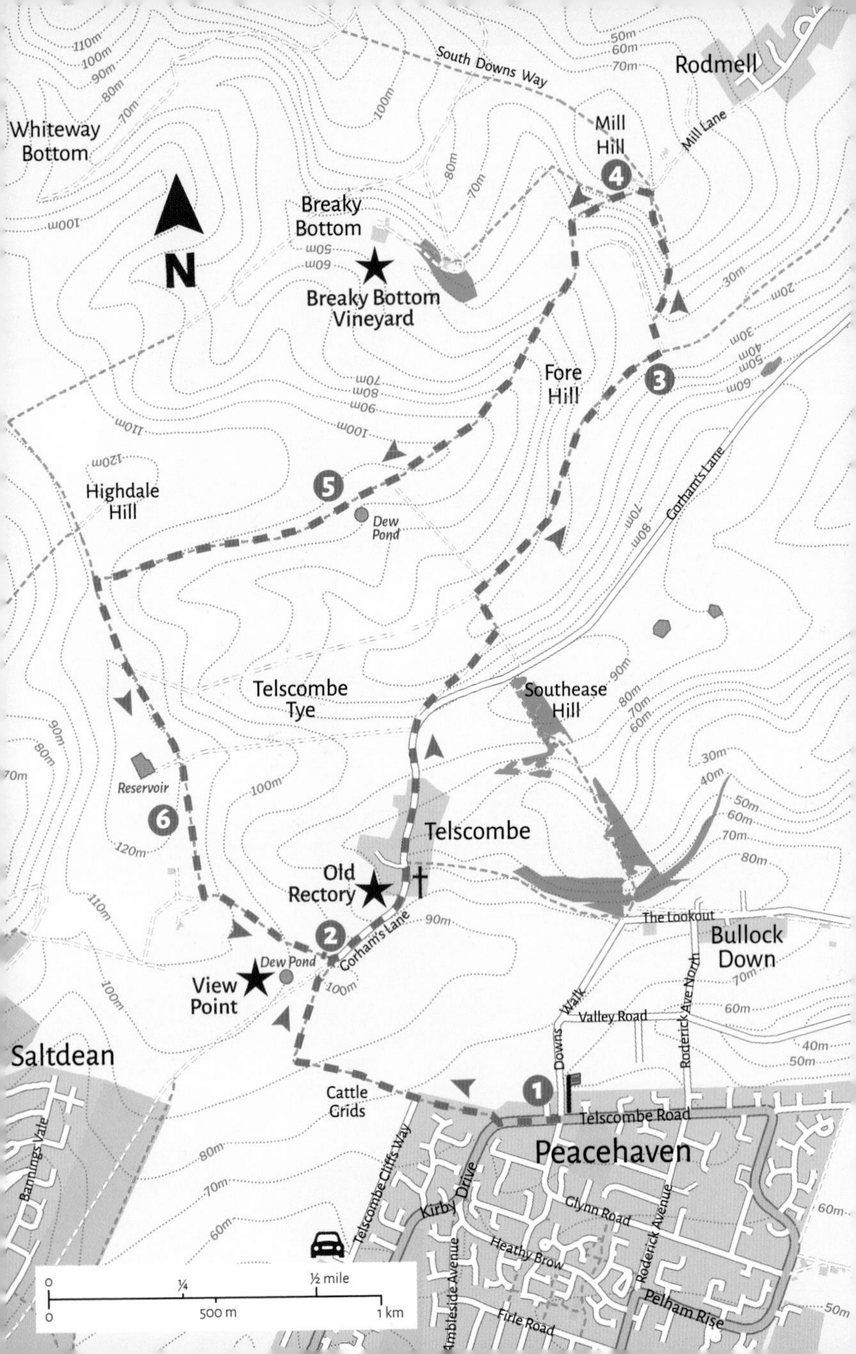
South Downs Way
Rodmell
Mill Lane
Mill Hill
Whiteway Bottom
Breaky Bottom
Breaky Bottom Vineyard
N
Fore Hill
Highdale Hill
Dew Pond
Gorham's Lane
Telscombe Tye
Southease Hill
Reservoir
Telscombe
Old Rectory
The Lookout
Bullock Down
View Point
Saltdean
Valley Road
Downs Walk
Roderick Ave North
Cattle Grids
Telscombe Road
Peacehaven
Telscombe Cliffs Way
Kirby Drive
Bannings Vale
Glynn Road
Heathy Brow
Roderick Avenue
Ambleside Avenue
Pelham Rise
Firle Road
1
2
3
4
5
6
0
¼
½ mile
0
500 m
1 km

❶ From the bus stop adjacent to Downs Walk on Telscombe Road, walk down to the bridleway which heads off in the same direction at the junction with Kirby Road. Follow the bridleway around the bend and past the cattle grid until you come to a gate. Follow the track round to the right until you reach a signpost.

❷ Walk down the road through Telscombe village, passing the church on your right and the Old Rectory on your left. Follow the road until you come to a bridleway on your left. Go through the gate and follow the bridleway down into the valley, following the track. Go through the gate and follow the track to the right. Keep on the track, following it down into the farmyard.

❸ When you come to a South Downs Way signpost ahead of you, turn left through the gate. Follow the path uphill through another gate and on to the gate at the top of the Mill Hill.

❹ Do not pass through this gate, but turn left following the footpath along the field edge down into the valley. Go through the next gate and head up the hill. You will see Breaky Bottom Vineyard on your right as you walk up the hill.

❺ Continue across the field, then keeping the dew pond and sheepfold to your left, head towards the centre of the field and towards a gate ahead. Go through this gate and across another field to a third gate, after which you turn left onto the bridleway which will take you on to Telscombe Tye.

❻ Go through the gate next to a reservoir and cross the fields through three more gates. There is a Dew Pond here, where you can stop and enjoy the view. Follow the bridleway back to the signpost at the top of the road and retrace your steps back to the bus stop.

WALK 10
Buriton

A lovely walk with some amazing scenery.

The pretty village of Buriton enjoys an idyllic location at the foot of the Downs. Known as a 'springline village', it owes its existence to its natural water supply.

The chalk in the surrounding hills acts like a giant sponge, absorbing rainwater and storing it in an underground aquifer. The water from the aquifer surfaces in the form of springs, which feed the streams and rivers in this area and provide drinking water to well over a million people on the south coast of England.

At Buriton, chalk was also extracted from the ground, leaving steep-sided 'quarry bowls'. Now abandoned, the Chalk Pits have regenerated and provide a rich habitat for a high level of chalk-based species. The site has been designated a Site of Importance for Nature Conservation (SINC) and a Local Nature Reserve.

This circular walk passes close to the Chalk Pits and follows part of the South Downs Way before returning to the village past Buriton House.

Distance: 3 miles (4.8 km)
Time: 1½–2 hours
Terrain: Steep hills and stiles.
Start/Finish: Bus stop on Buriton High Street (SU737202)
Nearest Postcode: GU31 5SG
Map: OS Explorer OL33 Haslemere & Petersfield

❶ From the bus stop turn right down the High Street passing the village school.

❷ Turn right at the pond onto South Lane and follow the bridleway under the railway bridge and up the hill.

❸ Halfway up the hill you can take a track off to the left, through the gate, to visit Buriton Chalk Pits. Retrace your footsteps back to the main path to continue the walk.

❹ At the crossroads turn left and follow the lane onto the South Downs Way (SDW).

❺ Follow the SDW past Coulters Dean Farm and onto the road where it bears round to the left.

❻ At the right-hand corner take the byway off to the left known as the Milky Way.

❼ Follow this track down the hill and around to the right, heading north.

❽ When the track meets Pitcroft Lane turn left.

❾ Just after the gates to Buriton House take the footpath to your left up some small steps.

❿ Follow the path past the big house and through a field until you join the road.

⓫ Follow the road back round to the pond and church, then retrace your footsteps along the High Street and back to the bus stop.

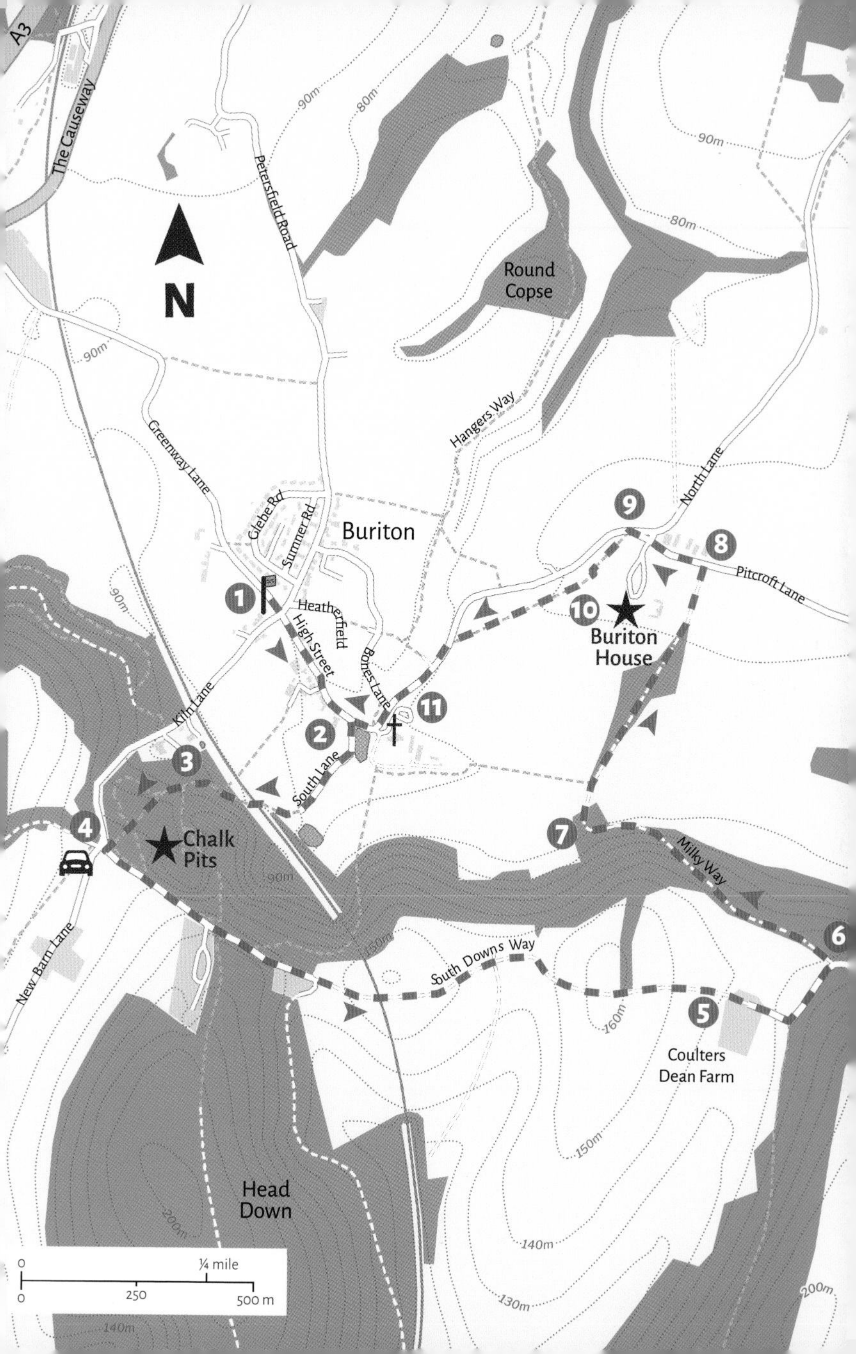
A3
The Causeway
Petersfield Road
N
Round
Copse
90m
80m
Hangers Way
Greenway Lane
Glebe Rd
Sumner Rd
Buriton
North Lane
9
8
Pitcroft Lane
1
Heatherfield
High Street
Bones Lane
10
Buriton
House
11
Kiln Lane
2
3
South Lane
4
Chalk
Pits
7
Milky Way
South Downs Way
6
5
Coulters
Dean Farm
New Barn Lane
150m
160m
Head
Down
200m
140m
130m
0
¼ mile
250
500 m

The hills around the village of Buriton are some of the highest in the South Downs.

WALK 11

Lewes and Glynde

Have your camera at the ready for this varied walk.

Lewes developed as a medieval port on the River Ouse, with related brewing, iron and ship-building industries. During the seventeenth and eighteenth centuries it flourished as the country town of Sussex.

The surrounding area can be explored on this circular walk, which takes you through some of the best chalk downland and wildlife-rich reserves that the National Park has to offer. Panoramic views across the South Downs, Ouse valley and Lewes are guaranteed!

❶ From the end of the station approach in Glynde, turn left along the road into the village and then left again along Ranscombe Lane, just past the Post Office.

❷ Almost immediately, go right through the gate and follow the footpath to a stile. Cross the stile and follow the footpath which climbs steadily up onto a shoulder of Mount Caburn.

❸ Where the path levels out, turn left along the fence line leading to the gate into the National Nature Reserve and the summit of Mount Caburn. Return to the route by retracing your steps to point 3 (see below for an optional shortcut) and turn left over the stile. Follow the unfenced path downhill and when you reach the field corner bear left over the stile into Southerham Nature Reserve. Follow the grassy path along the valley bottom.

Shortcut: Instead of crossing the stile when leaving Mount Caburn, go straight ahead alongside the fence for about 200 m. When you see a gate on the left, turn right down the unfenced track opposite, and rejoin the full walk directions at point 10.

4 Go through the gate next to the dew pond and climb diagonally up the side of the valley across the field. Beyond the next gate turn left on the path and climb uphill until you reach the gate to the Lewes Golf Club Clubhouse.

5 Pass to the left of the clubhouse.

6 Turn right down the access road to see panoramic views over Lewes. At the fork in the road, bear right along the rough track (or, to visit Lewes continue straight ahead downhill instead).

7 Turn right sharply up a steep flight of steps. Continue uphill and straight across the golf course (following waymark posts) – care is needed to keep to the path line and avoid golf balls when signs advise. Cross the stile onto open access land and continue.

8 Go through two gates and continue to the sky line at Saxon Down. Follow the track straight ahead, skirting the copse and on to the dew pond. Before reaching the gate, take a sharp right turn.

9 Go along the chalky track which passes to the left of an old quarry (with views of Glyndebourne Opera House to the left). Fork left, then go straight ahead through two gates and follow clear track across open downland where you will see point 3 in sight about 200 m ahead. Look out for a gate on the right, then turn left down the unfenced track opposite.

10 Follow the track downhill. At the bottom of the track, just before the buildings, follow the path left along the field boundary to a gate and steps down to the road. Turn right and follow the road past Glynde Place and Glynde Church back into the village, retracing your steps to the station.

Distance: 6½ miles (10.5 km)
Time: 4½ hours
Access: Hilly, some stiles.
Start/Finish: Glynde Station (TQ457086)
Nearest Postcode: BN8 6RU
Map: OS Explorer OL25 Eastbourne & Beachy Head

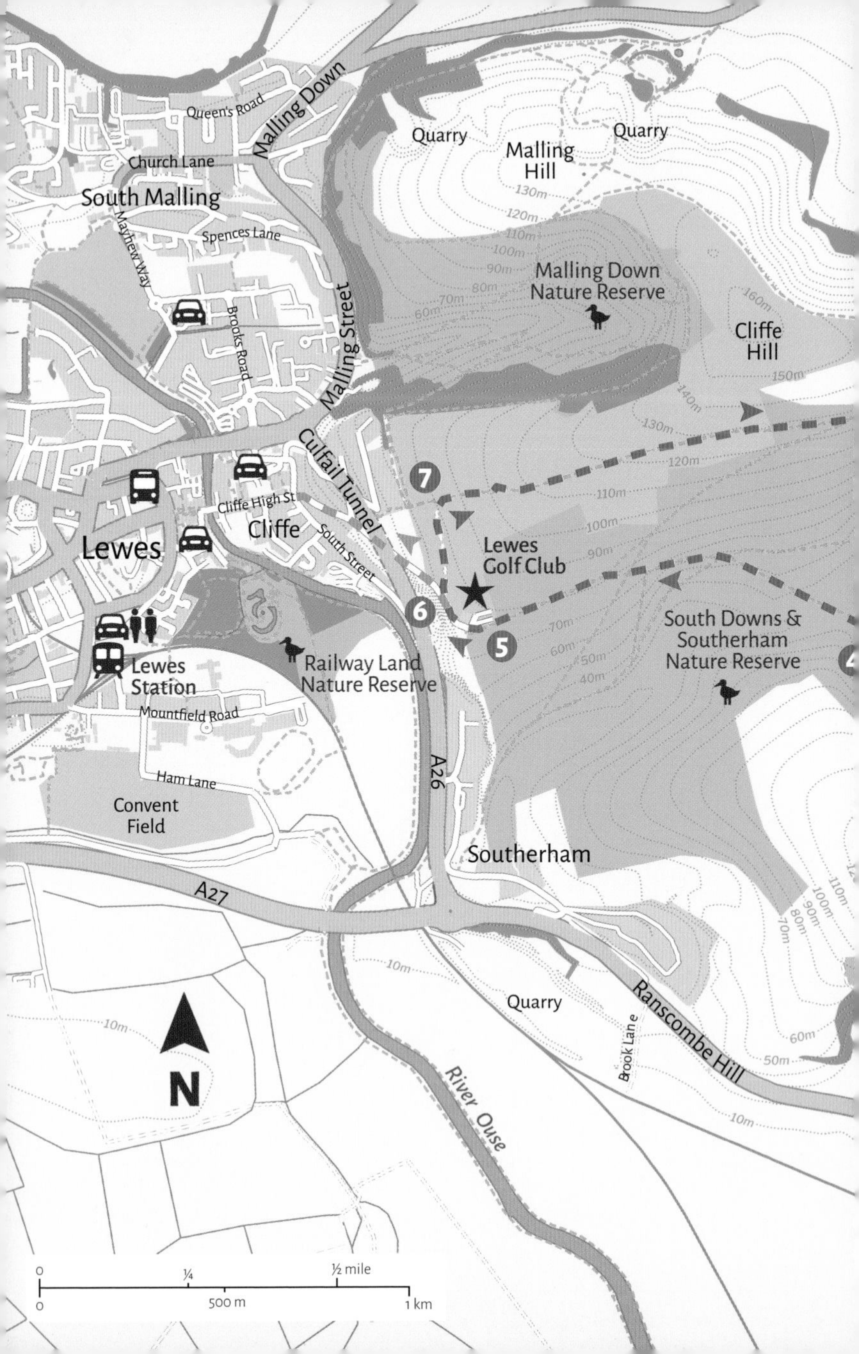
Queen's Road
Malling Down
Quarry
Quarry
Malling
Hill
Church Lane
South Malling
Mayhew Way
Spences Lane
130m
120m
110m
100m
90m
80m
70m
60m
Malling Down
Nature Reserve
160m
Cliffe
Hill
150m
140m
130m
120m
110m
100m
90m
70m
60m
50m
40m
Brooks Road
Malling Street
Culfail Tunnel
Cliffe High St
Cliffe
South Street
Lewes
7
6
5
Lewes
Golf Club
South Downs &
Southerham
Nature Reserve
Railway Land
Nature Reserve
Lewes
Station
Mountfield Road
Ham Lane
Convent
Field
A26
Southerham
A27
10m
Quarry
Ranscombe Hill
Brook Lane
River Ouse
10m
N
0
¼
½ mile
0
500 m
1 km

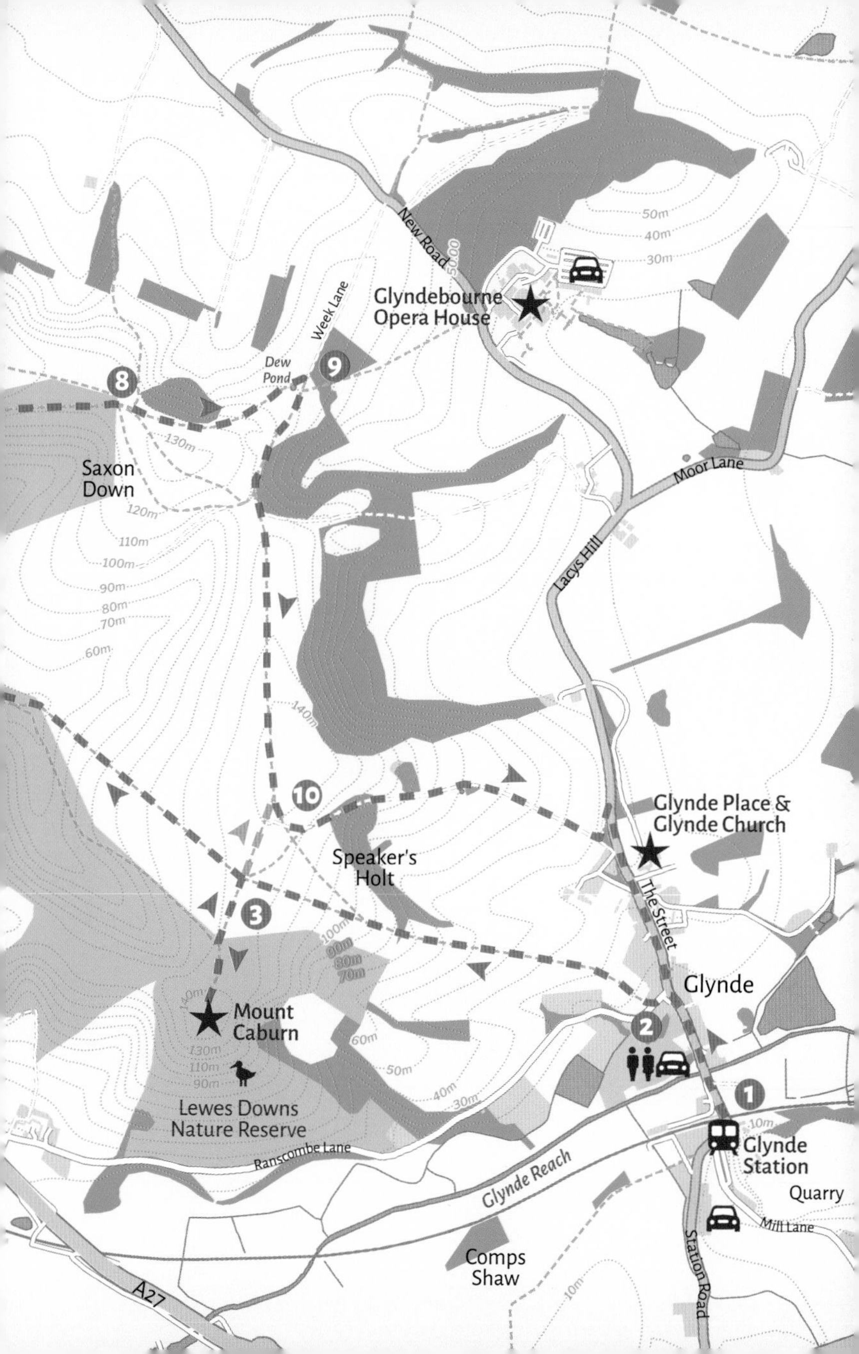

New Road
Week Lane
Glyndebourne Opera House
Dew Pond
Saxon Down
Moor Lane
Lacys Hill
Glynde Place & Glynde Church
Speaker's Holt
The Street
Glynde
Mount Caburn
Lewes Downs Nature Reserve
Ranscombe Lane
Glynde Reach
Glynde Station
Quarry
Mill Lane
Comps Shaw
Station Road
A27

WALK 12

Steyning, Chanctonbury and Washington

Steeped in history and offering breathtaking scenery, Cissbury and Chanctonbury Ring are integral to experiencing the South Downs National Park.

Steyning town is rich in history, with scores of timberframed buildings in and around the ancient high street. It was once a port on the River Adur and was prized by the Normans; their legacy today includes the magnificent parish church and the ruins of the castle in nearby Bramber. Visit some of the many shops, restaurants, pubs and tea rooms, or pop by for the monthly farmers' market. The route of this circular walk takes you out of Steyning and then steeply up to join the South Downs Way. You'll see views of Cissbury Ring, which covers 60 acres and is one of the largest Middle Iron Age hillforts in Europe. The earthworks date back to 250 BC.

The trail also takes you past Chanctonbury Ring, another Iron Age hillfort. The Ring's current fame stems from a crown of beech trees planted in 1750 by Charles Goring of Wiston House. Although not well received initially, the trees later became a well-known landmark.

Distance: 7 miles (11.3 km)
Time: 3–4 hours
Terrain: Moderately difficult circular walk with steep ascents.
Start/Finish: Steyning High Street (TQ177110)
Nearest Postcode: BN44 3GG
Map: OS Explorer OL11 Brighton & Hove and OS Explorer OL10 Arundel & Pulborough

London Road
A24
Quarry
The Hollow
Quarry
The Pike
Steynin
Water Lane
Chanctonbury Ring Road
School Ln
The Street
London Road
Washington
Plantefield
Chanctonbury
Ring
View
Point
Wiston Bostal
South Downs Way
Horsham Road
A24
6
5
4
0
¼
½ mile
500 m
1 km

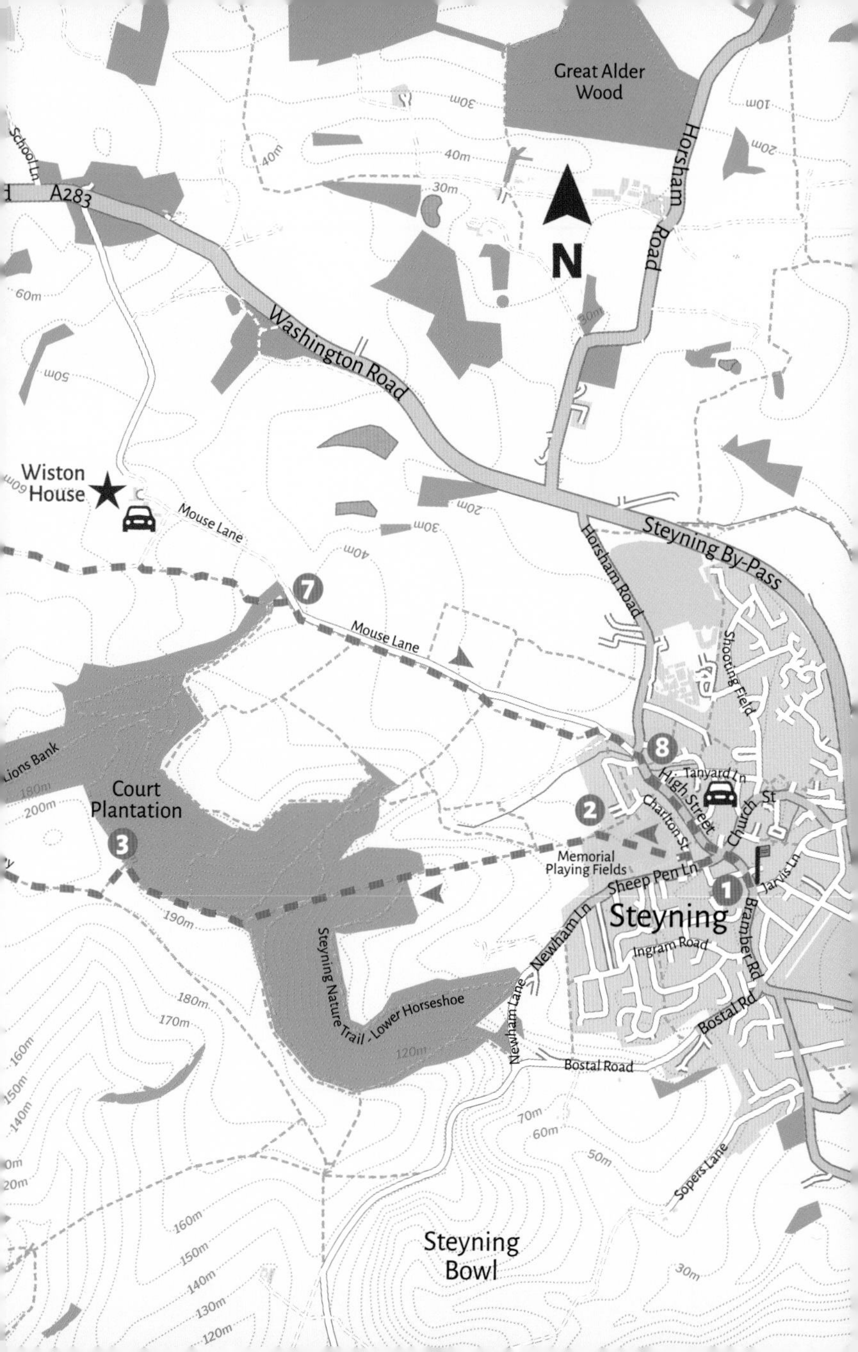

Great Alder Wood
Horsham Road
N
A283
School Ln
Washington Road
Wiston House
Mouse Lane
Steyning By-Pass
Horsham Road
Shooting Field
7
8
Mouse Lane
Tanyard Ln
High Street
Church St
Charlton St
2
Lions Bank
Court Plantation
3
Memorial Playing Fields
Sheep Pen Ln
1
Jarvis Ln
Steyning
Bramber Rd
Newham Ln
Ingram Road
Steyning Nature Trail - Lower Horseshoe
Newham Lane
Bostal Rd
Bostal Road
Sopers Lane
Steyning Bowl

❶ From the bus stop adjacent to Bramber Road in Steyning walk up the High Street and turn left at the roundabout onto Sheep Pen Lane. At White Horse Square, turn right. When you get to the police station, turn left and enter a playing field, then head to the far right corner.

❷ Go through a gate and turn left up a track. Pass through two more gates and enter a more open area. Continue straight ahead up a grassy slope going through another gate, and join another path coming up. Continue up the hill.

❸ At the edge of the woods, join another path that comes from the left, then keep the trees on your right. Ignore downhill paths and continue to the corner of the field. Follow the path to the left and then turn right onto the South Downs Way.

❹ To your left are views of Cissbury Ring and beyond to the coast. Follow the South Downs Way, keeping the trees on your right. At a gate and cattle grid, go straight ahead with Chanctonbury Ring clearly ahead of you.

❺ After Chanctonbury Ring, immediately turn half right, leaving the South Downs Way and walk down to a gate. Pass through the gate, and descend steeply down a grassy slope through woods.

❻ Stay on the path, passing through a gate and, after a short rise, descend to a junction of paths. Drop down to a lower path and turn right. Arriving at a small clearing with four gates, the left-hand field gate and smaller gate are the route to Washington. To the right is a pair of field gates. The right-hand gate into the woods is the route back to Steyning.

Optional diversion to Washington: To go to Washington, go through the small gate and bear half left across a field on a footpath (do not follow the track on the field edge). Cross a stile and walk straight on towards the right-hand side of the next field. Join a track and bear left on this track, to pass through a gate. Keep ahead on the grass when the track turns right into a farm. Ignore a side path and go straight ahead to the right corner and another stile. Descend via steps, then up to a stile and a road. Turn right and look out for the Frankland Arms pub in Washington. Return by retracing your steps to the clearing with 4 gates.

To return to Steyning, take the right-hand field gate into the woods. Just after another old gate post near the brow of a rise, you'll see a path coming in from the right. Ignore this path and continue on the main track, passing through an old iron field gate. Pass a house shortly before a minor road. Turn right, and then left, over a stile to pass some farm buildings, then continue behind Wiston House. Cross two stiles and go under a high footbridge. Where the tarmac turns left, keep right, and walk between trees and a fence, following the way to a stile.

7 Cross a tiny stream, and follow the path. At the field corner, you can either go ahead to turn right on a minor road (Mouse Lane) or turn right to walk along the path parallel with Mouse Lane. You can access Mouse Lane at several points along this path, but if you continue over a stile and steps, turn left at the next path which crosses to join Mouse Lane.

8 At the end of Mouse Lane, join the High Street and continue straight ahead to return to the start point.

WALK 13

Haslemere to Liphook

There are fewer more beautiful sights in the world than a South Downs heath in full summer bloom.

Heathlands are one of the most unique – and threatened – habitats in the country. Those on the South Downs are particularly special, developing into a thick carpet of pinks and purples that make for some breathtaking scenery.

Beneath this blanket of colour is a rich biodiversity. Lowland heath is home to some of Britain's rarest wildlife, including all twelve native reptiles and amphibians. You'll be lucky to see a snake, even on the hottest summer's day, but you may see a bright green sand lizard. Look carefully and you may see a Dartford warbler foraging for bugs.

This pleasant linear walk between the towns of Haslemere and Liphook gives you the opportunity to explore the heathland of Marley, Lynchmere and Stanley Commons. Both towns have stations on the main London Waterloo line, so you can return to Haslemere by train.

Distance: 5 miles (8 km)
Time: 3 hours (non-circular)
Terrain: Some steep climbs and one steep descent. Uneven surfaces – take care crossing or walking along roads. One stile.
Start: Haslemere Station (SU898329)
Nearest Postcode: GU27 2PD
Map: OS Explorer OL33 Haslemere & Petersfield

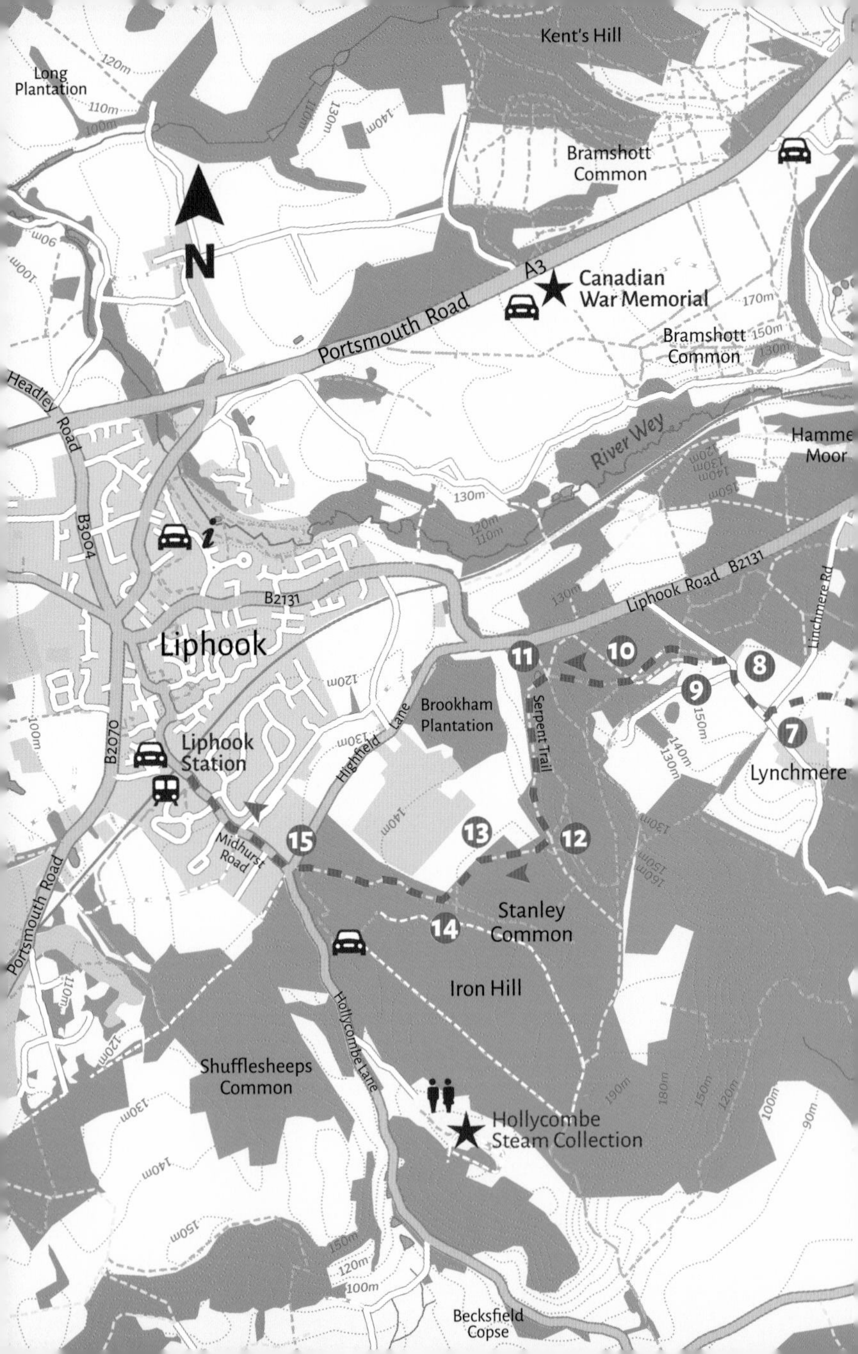
Kent's Hill
Long Plantation
Bramshott Common
N
Canadian War Memorial
Portsmouth Road
A3
Bramshott Common
Headley Road
River Wey
Hammer Moor
B3004
Liphook Road B2131
Linchmere Rd
B2131
Liphook
Brookham Plantation
Serpent Trail
Lynchmere
B2070
Liphook Station
Highfield Lane
Midhurst Road
Portsmouth Road
Stanley Common
Iron Hill
Hollycombe Lane
Shufflesheeps Common
Hollycombe Steam Collection
Becksfield Copse
1
2
3
4
5
6
7
8
9
10
11
12
13
14
15

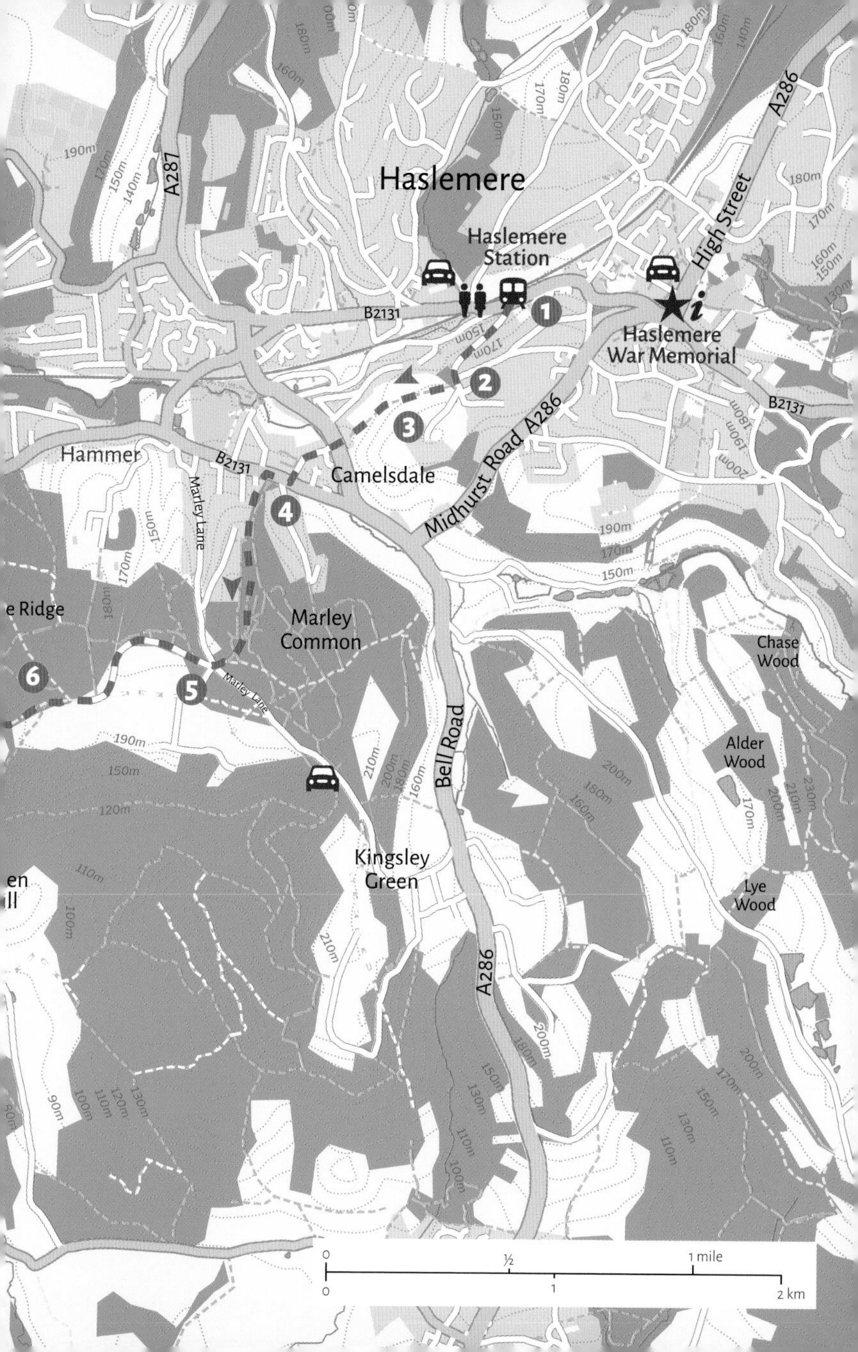

Haslemere
Haslemere Station
Haslemere War Memorial
High Street
A286
A287
B2131
Midhurst Road A286
Hammer
Camelsdale
Marley Lane
Marley Common
e Ridge
Bell Road
Kingsley Green
Chase Wood
Alder Wood
Lye Wood
en
ill
1
2
3
4
5
6
0
½
1 mile
1
2 km

1 At Haslemere, leave the train station forecourt and cross into Longdene Road opposite. Climb this residential street and keep straight on at the bend into Hedgehog Lane.

2 Turn right onto a footpath opposite a house called Ridgeways. Continue through a gate and cross a field, then take the stile by Sturt Farm to join the road.

3 Cross the road diagonally to the right, go through railings and down a steep path onto residential Sturt Ave. Continue to the T-junction and turn right. Cross the road to the bus shelter.

4 Turn right and then turn left at the fingerpost. Head uphill on a steep wooded footpath to Marley Common, continuing straight on at the first and second marker posts. You are now within the South Downs National Park. At the third marker post bear right and go through a gate marked '3'. Continue on to a five-bar gate.

5 Go through the gate and cross a multi-lane junction, bearing right onto a tarmac lane marked as the Serpent Trail. Follow the path straight ahead, passing the Lynchmere Society information board which is worth a read.

6 Pass a sign for 'Harboury' house and continue on the wooded Sussex Border Path until you reach a tarmac lane.

7 Cross over the lane and the grassy triangle, and bear right onto the road (heading towards Liphook).

8 Walk along the road. Pass Danley Lane on the left and then bearing left, go through a five-bar gate and follow the Sussex Border Path onto Lynchmere Common.

9 The Sussex Border Path joins the Serpent Trail. Turn right at the next finger post (with some cattle pens on your right). As you enter the open common turn left and follow the power lines for three posts.

10 Continue past a turning to the right and then bear right through some birch trees to a marker post for the Sussex Border Path. Continue on this rough path through the heath to the bottom of the hill.

11 Bear left before the five-bar gate to a wooden bench by a spring-fed pond. The path climbs here. Continue straight on at the fingerpost and keep going alongside the fence on an undulating path, still on the Sussex Border Path/Serpent Trail.

12 Turn right at a four-way junction, climbing uphill. Bear right at the top onto a wide track, which soon becomes well surfaced.

13 Don't cross the cattle grid. Turn left at the Serpent Trail sign and go downhill to the Lynchmere Society information board 'Stanley Common'.

14 At the sign turn right through the gate. Continue along the path and soon rejoin the Sussex Border Path until you reach the road. Turn left and walk the few steps to the junction.

15 To finish at Liphook Station turn right and follow Midhurst Road along the pavement for 0.6 miles (1 km). Take the footbridge over the railway and turn right down some steps to the station.

WALK 14

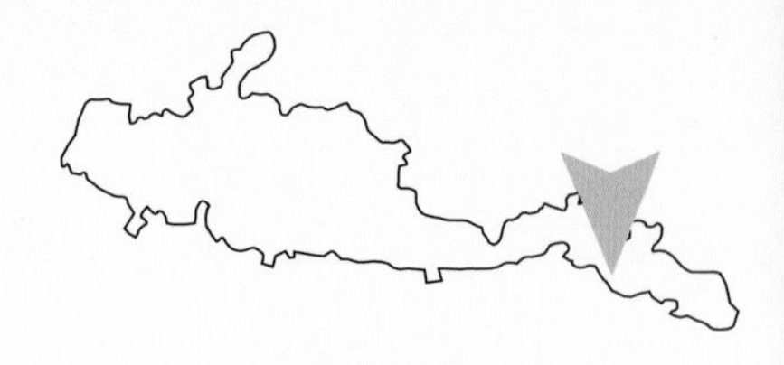

Rottingdean

Walking in the footsteps of Kipling, you can see exactly why he was so inspired by the South Downs.

This walk will take you across a small part of the 'whale-backed Downs' that *The Jungle Book* author Rudyard Kipling loved so much. After staying in Rottingdean as a young boy, the author decided to settle in the village as an adult.

Others who have found inspiration roaming the Downs around Rottingean include writers Virginia Woolf, Katherine Mansfield, D. H. Lawrence, Oscar Wilde, Enid Bagnold and Angela Thirkell, while movie stars like Bette Davis, Errol Flynn, Cary Grant and Julie Andrews enjoyed stays at the Tudor Close Hotel. Following in their footsteps with the wide sky above and the pewter sea below may bring to mind Kipling's personal tribute to the Downs:

> *God gives all men all earth to love,*
> *But, since man's heart is small,*
> *Ordains for each one spot shall prove*
> *Beloved over all.*
> *Each to his choice, and I rejoice*
> *The lot has fallen to me*
> *In a fair ground – in a fair ground –*
> *Yea, Sussex by the sea!*

Distance: 3 miles (4.8 km)
Time: 2 hours
Terrain: Mix of road, track and grassland. Easy with moderate inclines, rolling downs and muddy in places.
Start/Finish: Rottingdean War Memorial (TQ368025)
Nearest Postcode: BN2 7HA
Map: OS Explorer OL11 Brighton & Hove

Woodingdean
N
Balsdean Reservoir
Balsdean Farm
Ovingdean
Falmer Road B2123
Bazehill Road
Dean Court Road
Whiteway Lane
Bishopstone Drive
Lustrells Vale
Westmeston Avenue
Beacon Hill
St Margaret's
War Memorial
Beacon Mill
St Martha's Convent
The Grange
Rottingdean
Saltdean
Marine Drive
Undercliff Walk
Marine Drive
A259
1
2
3
4
5
120m
110m
100m
90m
80m
70m
60m
50m
40m
0
¼ mile
0
250
500 m

❶ From the war memorial and village green, cross the road to St Margaret's Church, turn left and walk two streets up to Bazehill Road.

❷ Turn right and follow uphill as the road becomes a single lane and leads to panaromic views of the open downland, Beacon Mill and the English Channel.

❸ The route dips, revealing the beautiful Balsdean valley. Then halfway down take a sharp right turn, through a gate opposite a farm track. Go south along the grass path, through a second gate, and along the edge of the field, on the far side of the Balsdean Farm buildings. Go through a third gate and walk straight through more open farmland with views towards Saltdean.

❹ At the bottom of the fields, the path cuts between two houses and out onto Bishopstone Drive. Look left into Lustrell's Vale where Kipling set up a training rifle range in 1898. Turn right into Whiteway Lane, leading back down to the village and at the bottom, turn right.

❺ At The Grange, once the vicarage, turn right to return to the war memorial, facing Kipling's house, The Elms. Look left across The Green to Prospect Cottage and Aubrey House, where Kipling's aunt Georgina and Edward Burne-Jones, the Pre-Raphaelite painter, lived, worked and first welcomed Kipling to the village.

WALK 15
Harting

Look out for the copper green tower of St Gabriel Church on this scenic walk.

The rural parish of Harting sits at the foot of the Downs on the northern side and offers some spectacular scenery. The parish consists of the village of South Harting and the hamlets of West Harting, East Harting and Nyewood.

The parish church of St Mary and St Gabriel is in South Harting. Its distinctive green coppered tower is one of the major landmarks of the Rother valley and can be spotted from the tops of the nearby Downs, standing out amongst the picturesque Georgian cottages.

This circular walk starts near the church in South Harting and takes a circular route through the three hamlets of the parish.

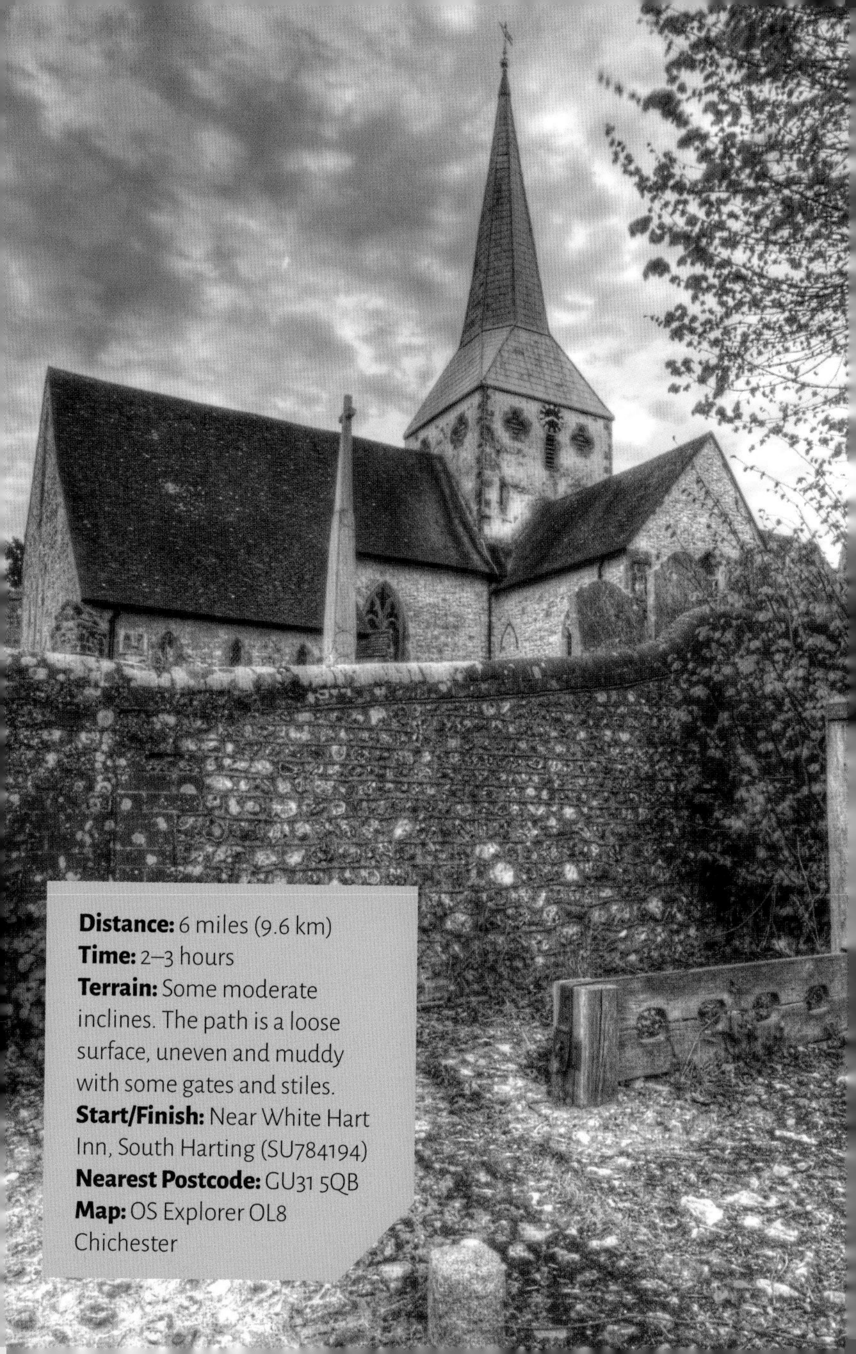

Distance: 6 miles (9.6 km)
Time: 2–3 hours
Terrain: Some moderate inclines. The path is a loose surface, uneven and muddy with some gates and stiles.
Start/Finish: Near White Hart Inn, South Harting (SU784194)
Nearest Postcode: GU31 5QB
Map: OS Explorer OL8 Chichester

1 From the bus stop outside the White Hart Inn in South Harting, walk north up the road taking the road straight ahead past Harting Stores and then right onto the public footpath.

2 Just before the copse, the footpath splits. Take the path to the left across the open field and over the footbridge. Follow the path to Tye Oak Farm where you will join the lane following it round to the left before finding your next footpath on the right to Nyewood.

3 When you reach the road at Nyewood turn left. Continue down the road then take the first footpath on the right opposite the park and between the houses.

4 After following the edge of several fields the footpath splits at the hedge line, take the left-hand path, going back on yourself across the fields. At the next open field head up the rise to a farm track and turn right towards Quebec.

5 From the lane past Hill Ash Farm you will reach the road. Turn left and walk along the quiet lane, bearing left at the top. Follow the lane until you come to a footpath on the right. Take this path along the field.

6 Carefully cross the B2146 at the junction. Walk up the driveway and turn left onto the footpath before the house to continue back into South Harting to the bus stop.

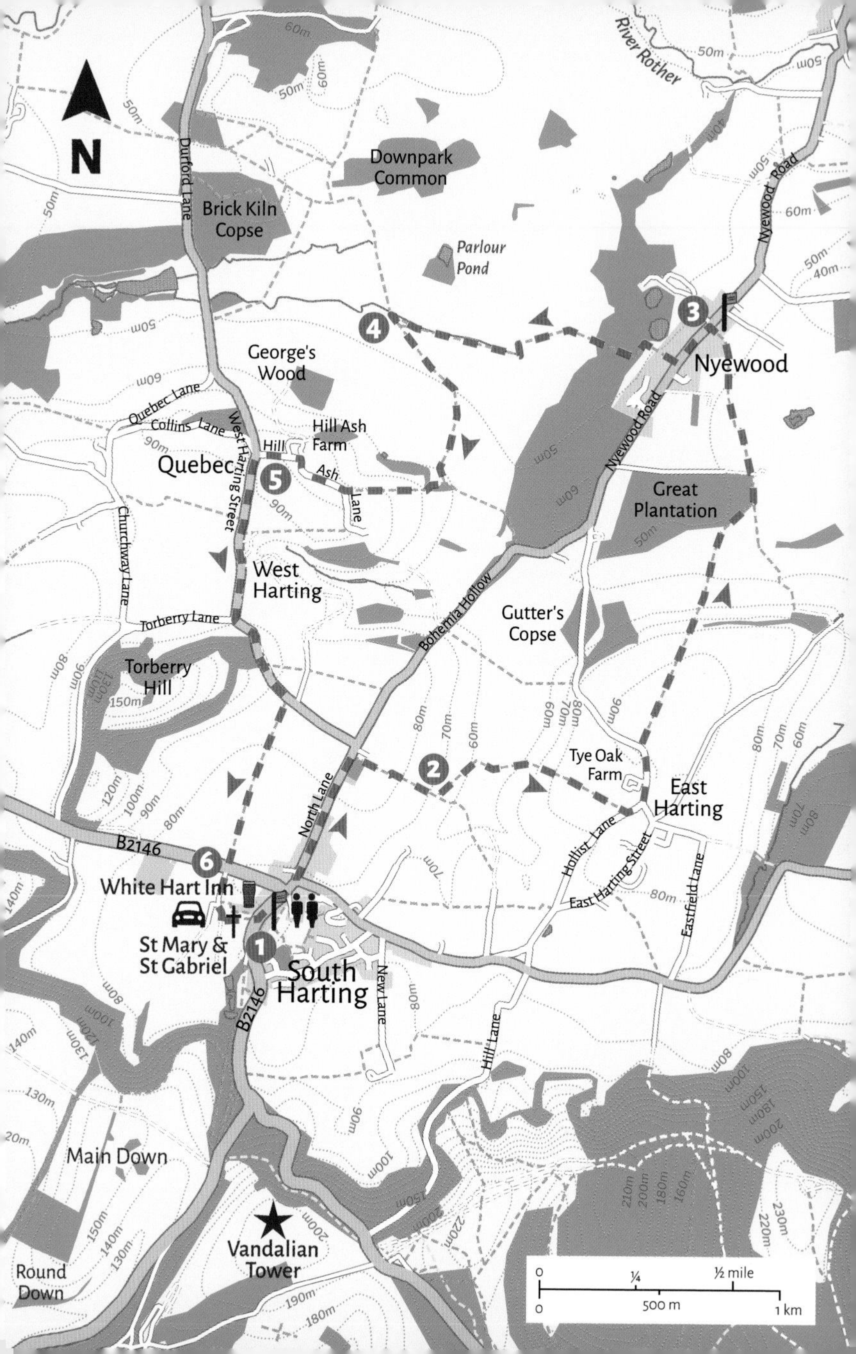

N
River Rother
Downpark Common
Brick Kiln Copse
Durford Lane
Parlour Pond
Nyewood Road
Nyewood
George's Wood
Quebec Lane
Collins Lane
West Harting Street
Hill Ash Farm
Hill
Ash
Lane
Quebec
Great Plantation
Churchway Lane
West Harting
Bohemia Hollow
Gutter's Copse
Torberry Lane
Torberry Hill
North Lane
Tye Oak Farm
East Harting
B2146
Hollist Lane
East Harting Street
Eastfield Lane
White Hart Inn
St Mary & St Gabriel
South Harting
New Lane
Hill Lane
Main Down
Vandalian Tower
Round Down
0
¼
½ mile
0
500 m
1 km

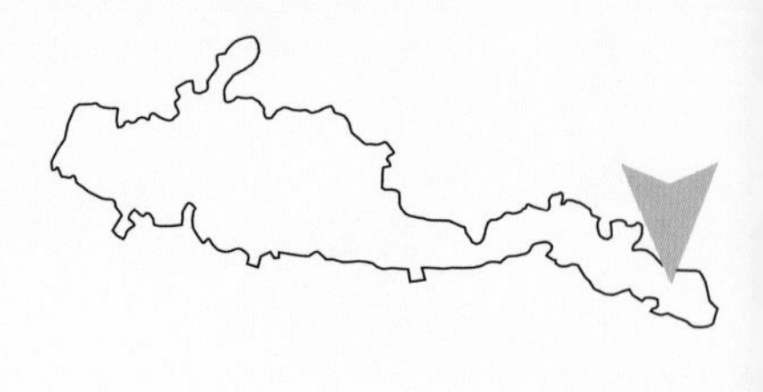

WALK 16

Alfriston and the Cuckmere Valley

The Cuckmere valley will certainly leave a long-lasting impression – it's so very beautiful.

One of the oldest villages in the country, Alfriston lies in the heart of the Cuckmere valley. It takes its name from the Anglo-Saxon Aelfric tun, meaning the 'farmstead of Alfric'. The village was recorded in the Domesday Book and the area is thought to have been occupied since Neolithic times as a number of long barrows can be found in the surrounding Downs. During the Napoleonic Wars at the beginning of the nineteenth century, Alfriston was home to a large number of troops stationed to repel any invaders who got past the Martello towers and cliffs on the coast. Following these wars, the village turned to smuggling, and the Alfriston Gang, well known for their violence, used the Cuckmere river to transport illegal goods in to the village.

This circular walk explores the southern part of the Cuckmere valley between the Seven Sisters Country Park and Alfriston. A highlight is the Litlington White Horse, a chalk figure carved in 1924 by a man called John T Ade, allegedly overnight by the light of a full moon so as to startle the locals with the sudden appearance of the horse in the morning!

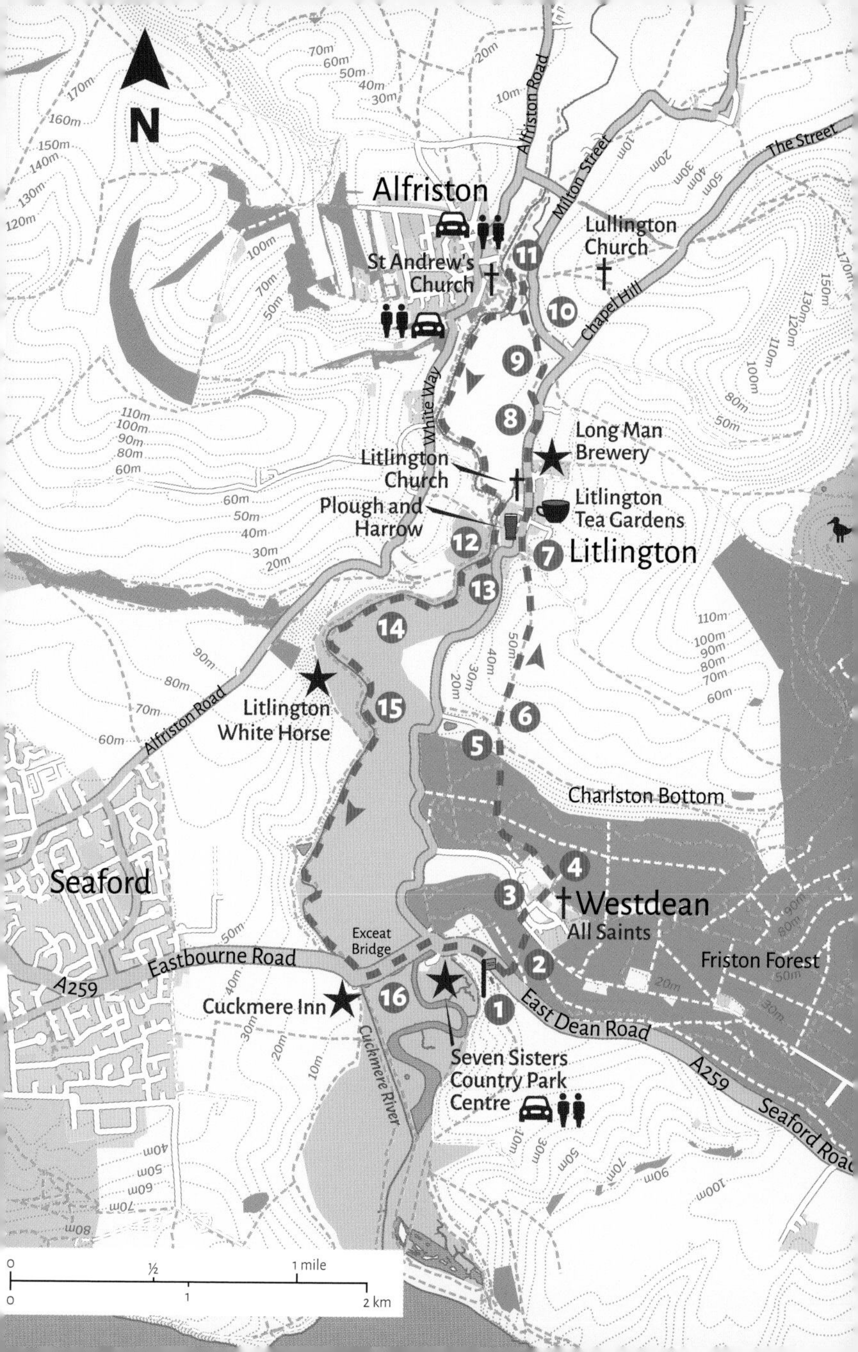
N
Alfriston
St Andrew's Church
Lullington Church
Alfriston Road
Milton Street
The Street
Chapel Hill
White Way
Long Man Brewery
Litlington Church
Plough and Harrow
Litlington Tea Gardens
Litlington
Litlington White Horse
Alfriston Road
Charlston Bottom
Seaford
Westdean
All Saints
Friston Forest
Exceat Bridge
Eastbourne Road
A259
Cuckmere Inn
East Dean Road
A259
Seaford Road
Seven Sisters Country Park Centre
Cuckmere River
0
½
1 mile
0
1
2 km

Distance: 6.4 miles (10.3 km)
Time: 4½ hours
Terrain: Several short steep climbs. A mix of quiet roads, forest tracks and uneven foot-paths with several stiles.
Start/Finish: Seven Sisters Country Park Centre (TV517993)
Nearest Postcode: BN25 4AB
Map: OS Explorer OL25 Eastbourne & Beachy Head

❶ From the bus stop at the Seven Sisters Country Park Centre, carefully cross the A259 and turn right. With the cycle hire barn on your left, follow the South Downs Way (SDW) signs through the kissing gate and up the hill.

❷ At the top of the hill, cross over the wall into Friston Forest and down a series of steps to the village of Westdean.

❸ With Westdean pond on your left, follow the SDW signs straight on, past some houses and uphill back into Friston Forest.

❹ Turn left at the path junction and follow the SDW signs through the forest until you reach a set of steps.

❺ Go down the steps and follow the SDW round to the left.

❻ Turn right at the path junction, cross the stile and follow the SDW/Vanguard Way uphill, over the brow and down into Litlington village.

❼ Turn left at the kissing gate behind the village hall and then right into Litlington. Walk through the village passing the Plough and Harrow pub, Litlington Tea Gardens, Litlington Church and Church Farm where the Long Man Brewery is based (not open to the public).

❽ At a property called 'The Ham', take the raised public footpath on the left side of the road. After 200 m branch left over a stile into a field and follow the field edge footpath.

❾ Cross the stile and follow the footpath diagonally left. Cross a second stile near Lullington Road and bear left.

❿ Go through the kissing gate and, keeping the fence on your right, follow the footpath to the corner of the field. Cross the stile and after 60 m turn left onto the SDW bridleway to the White Bridge at Alfriston. (To visit nearby Lullington Church, reputed to be the smallest church in Sussex, instead of turning left onto the SDW, turn right to reach Lullington Road. At the road edge, turn right then almost immediately left and follow the public footpath up behind Plonk Barn. Keep straight ahead at the path junction and follow the footpath through the trees. At the back of the house turn left up a narrow surfaced path to reach the church. Return via the same route, enjoying the beautiful views down the valley).

11 Before the bridge, turn left through a kissing gate, following the SDW/Vanguard Way with the river on your right. (To visit Alfriston village cross the White Bridge.) Continue for 1.1 miles (1.8 km), passing through a series of kissing gates until you reach Litlington.

12 At the SDW path junction continue straight ahead along the tarmac path to Litlington Bridge. Carry straight on with the Cuckmere river on your right to a kissing gate.

13 Go through the kissing gate and follow the riverbank footpath for almost half a mile.

14 At the path junction carry straight on and follow the riverbank footpath. Look up to your right to see the Litlington White Horse on the High and Over hill.

15 After 0.6 miles (1 km), continue straight on at the path junction, following the meandering riverside path for a further mile (1.6 km) over a series of stiles to the A259 at Exceat Bridge.

16 Cross the A259 and either turn left, following the pavement to return to Seven Sisters Country Park Centre, or finish at the bus stop at Exceat Bridge by The Cuckmere Inn.

WALK 17

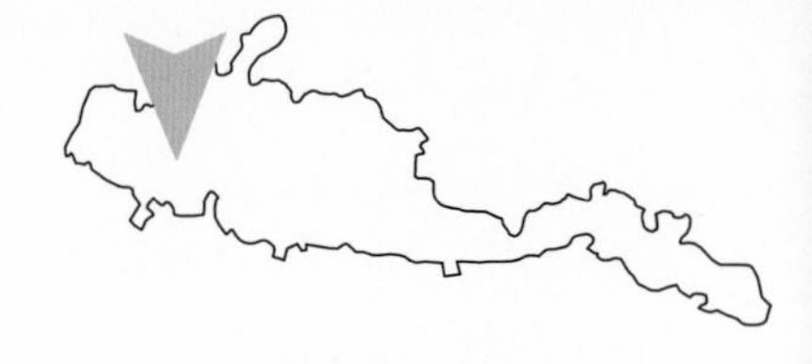

Meon Valley

This flat, wide walk along a disused railway line is perfect for families.

The Meon Valley Railway was built to transport agricultural produce, livestock and people along its 22½-mile (36-km) length. Following its final closure in 1968, an accessible trail has been created along a 10-mile (16-km) stretch between West Meon and Wickham, providing the opportunity for a fascinating walk through the history of the area.

The centrepiece of the valley is the River Meon, a rare natural chalk stream whose crystal-clear waters have been filtered through the chalk for thousands of years. The river attracts an abundance of wildlife, including otters, water voles, brown trout, kingfishers and plants such as water crowfoot.

West Meon has a rich history dating back to the Iron and Bronze Ages, with evidence of the Meonwara tribe and remains of a substantial Roman villa. At the other end of the trail, Wickham boasts one of the largest squares in the country, covering almost two acres.

Although the entire trail spans 10 miles (16 km), it is possible to walk, or cycle, shorter sections of it. It may also be followed in the opposite direction, but would take longer to complete due to being uphill.

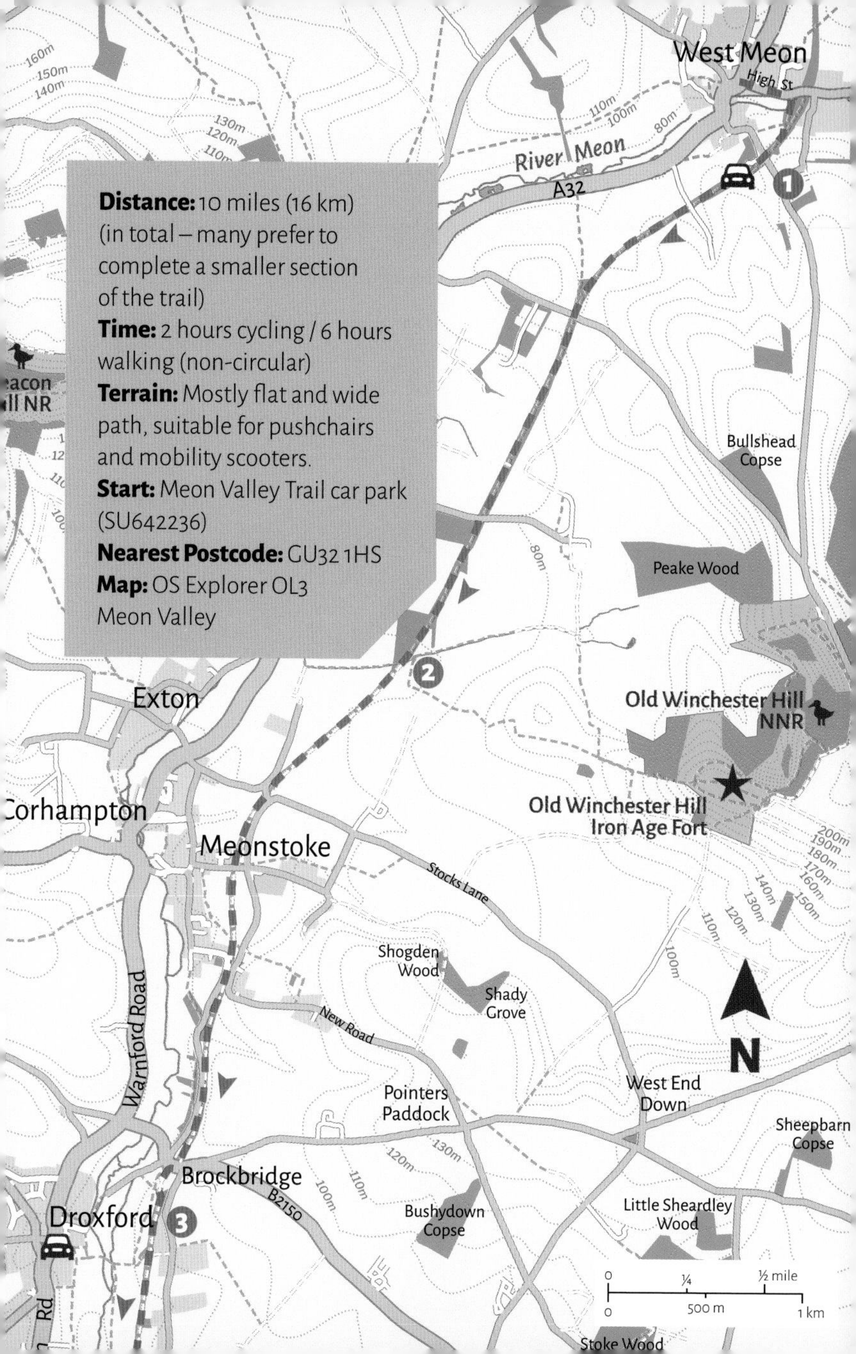
Distance: 10 miles (16 km)
(in total – many prefer to complete a smaller section of the trail)
Time: 2 hours cycling / 6 hours walking (non-circular)
Terrain: Mostly flat and wide path, suitable for pushchairs and mobility scooters.
Start: Meon Valley Trail car park (SU642236)
Nearest Postcode: GU32 1HS
Map: OS Explorer OL3 Meon Valley
West Meon
High St
River Meon
A32
1
2
3
Bullshead Copse
Peake Wood
Old Winchester Hill NNR
Old Winchester Hill Iron Age Fort
Exton
Corhampton
Meonstoke
Stocks Lane
Shogden Wood
Shady Grove
New Road
Warnford Road
Pointers Paddock
West End Down
Sheepbarn Copse
Brockbridge
B2150
Droxford
Bushydown Copse
Little Sheardley Wood
Stoke Wood
N
0
¼
½ mile
500 m
1 km

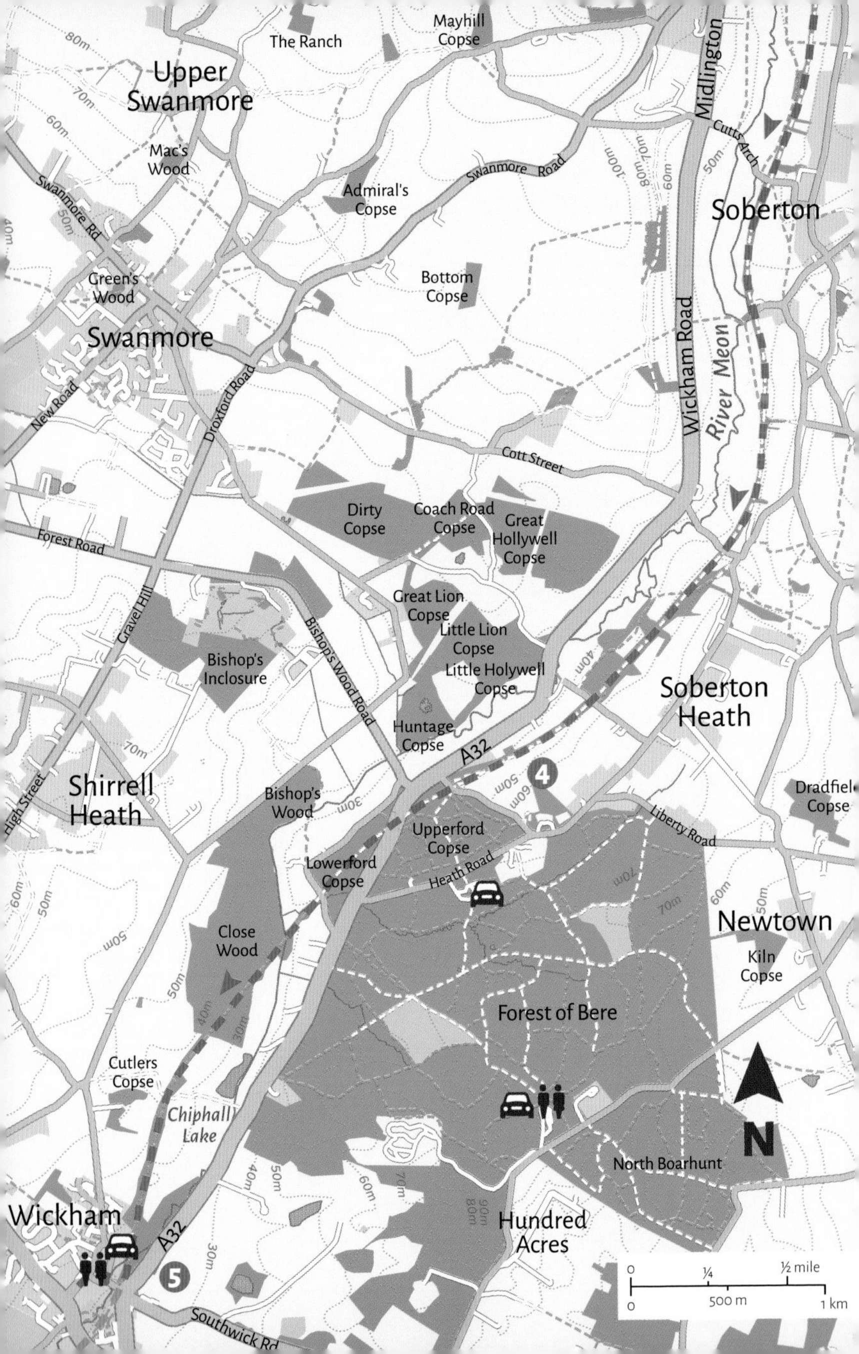

The Ranch
Mayhill Copse
Upper Swanmore
Midlington
Cutts Arch
Mac's Wood
Swanmore Road
Admiral's Copse
Soberton
Swanmore Rd
Green's Wood
Bottom Copse
Swanmore
Wickham Road
River Meon
Droxford Road
New Road
Cott Street
Dirty Copse
Coach Road Copse
Great Hollywell Copse
Forest Road
Great Lion Copse
Little Lion Copse
Little Holywell Copse
Gravel Hill
Bishop's Inclosure
Bishop's Wood Road
Soberton Heath
Huntage Copse
A32
Shirrell Heath
High Street
Bishop's Wood
Upperford Copse
Liberty Road
Dradfiel Copse
Lowerford Copse
Heath Road
Newtown
Close Wood
Kiln Copse
Forest of Bere
Cutlers Copse
Chiphall Lake
N
North Boarhunt
Wickham
Hundred Acres
Southwick Rd
0
¼
½ mile
500 m
1 km

❶ All users may start from the car park off Station Road in West Meon. Walkers can also use the footpath link from the High Street. Following the signpost to Wickham, head south on the trail, passing between the former station platforms.

❷ The trail takes you past Old Winchester Hill Iron Age fort, which encloses Bronze Age burial mounds, or barrows. The site was also used as a mortar testing range by the British Army during the Second World War. On the opposite side is Beacon Hill, a designated National Nature Reserve.

❸ Droxford station played a part in the D-Day preparations during the Second World War, as it was where prime minister Winston Churchill and his war cabinet arrived on the Royal train to meet with other leaders for secret discussions of the final plans for the invasion. The station building is now used as a private residence.

❹ Look out for signs of the abandoned goods yard at Mislingford, where a goods-only depot handled wood for the saw mill next door, and market garden produce from the local area. There are sleepers still in the ground and the remains of an iron crane can be seen.

❺ The trail ends at Wickham. To access the town centre, exit the trail into the car park on your right. Leave the car park, turn left onto Mill Lane and continue until you reach the town centre.

Optional: If you wish to proceed along the trail without stopping in Wickham, the path continues for another mile to Knowle.

The River Meon is one of the most untouched chalk streams in the South Downs.

WALK 18

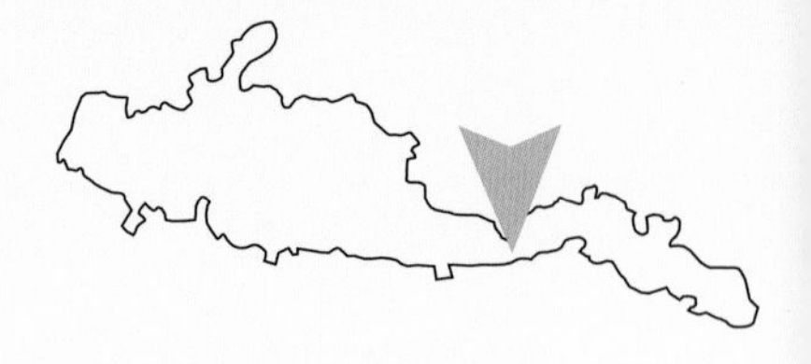

Mill Hill

Binoculars are a must for this lovely walk!

Mill Hill and the Adur valley are a wildlife-watcher's dream.

Mill Hill contains one of the few remaining areas of unimproved chalk grassland, which provides a rich and diverse habitat for an abundance of species. It has over half the British butterfly species and 160 different species of plant, and its importance has been recognized in its designation as a Site of Nature Conservation Importance (SNCI) and a Local Nature Reserve.

At the valley bottom, the River Adur widens as it nears the sea. This section is tidal, and becomes particularly interesting at mid-tide when the mud-flats appear, attracting many wading birds. Look out for ringed plovers, lapwings and little egrets.

This non-circular walk takes you from Shoreham-by-Sea up the river valley and around Mill Hill, passing through the nature reserve along the way.

Distance: 4½ miles (7.25 km)
Time: 2½ hours (non-circular)
Terrain: Mostly flat, grassy bridleways, uneven in places.
Start: Red Lion pub (TQ208056)
Nearest Postcode: BN43 5TE
Map: OS Explorer OL11 Brighton & Hove

❶ From the bus stop at the Red Lion pub, take St Nicholas Lane until you get to The Street; turn left and head up the hill. Take the footpath signposted to the left and follow it around the field. Continue up to the bridge that crosses the A27. Look out for the great views across the Adur valley.

❷ Cross the bridge and at the end take the footpath to the left. Follow this round to Mill Hill Nature Reserve and then take the footpath down the hill. Continue past Old Erringham Farm and back up onto the road.

❸ Turn right and head south along the road until you reach the track on the left-hand side that leads to New Erringham Farm. Follow the road past the farm and round to Mossy Bottom Barn.

❹ Leaving the track a short distance east of the barn, turn right and continue down towards Slonk Hill Farm.

❺ Cross the bridge over the A27 and continue on the track round to the vehicle entrance to the shopping centre.

❻ Carefully cross the road and use the pedestrian route into the car park. The walk ends at the bus stop, located at the south end of the covered walkway.

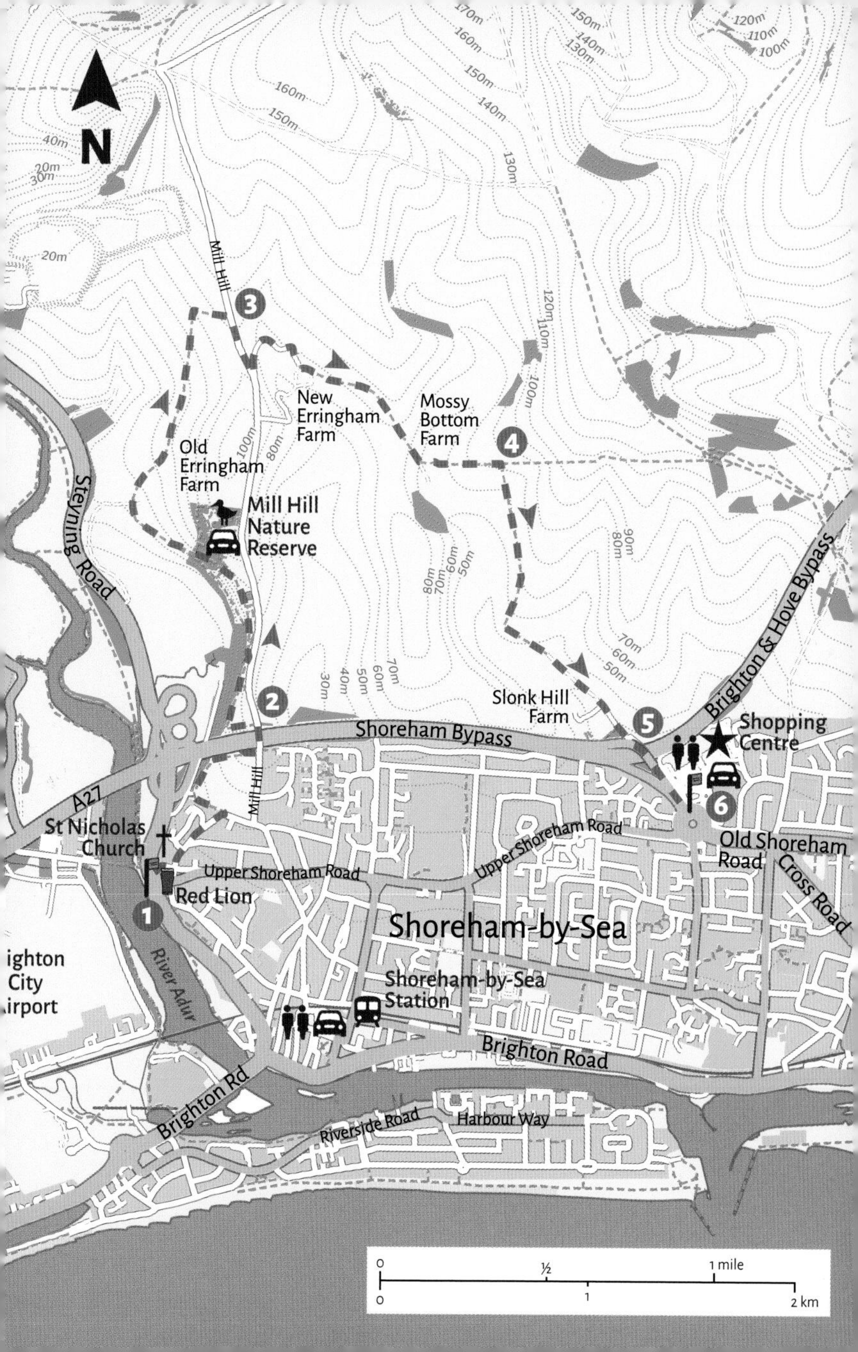
N
Mill Hill
New
Erringham
Farm
Mossy
Bottom
Farm
Old
Erringham
Farm
Mill Hill
Nature
Reserve
Steyning Road
Slonk Hill
Farm
Shoreham Bypass
Brighton & Hove Bypass
Shopping
Centre
A27
St Nicholas
Church
Red Lion
Upper Shoreham Road
Old Shoreham
Road
Cross Road
Shoreham-by-Sea
River Adur
ighton
City
irport
Shoreham-by-Sea
Station
Brighton Road
Brighton Rd
Riverside Road
Harbour Way
0
½
1 mile
0
1
2 km

Mill Hill provides panoramic views across the River Adur to the impressive Gothic chapel at Lancing College and over the town of Worthing to the English Channel beyond.

WALK 19

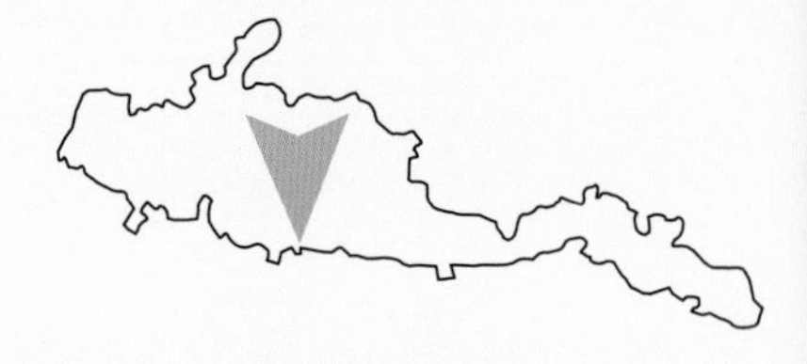

Centurion Way

This walk along a former railway line takes in city and country.

Connecting the historic cathedral city of Chichester and the picturesque village of West Dean, the Centurion Way – so-named because it crosses the course of a Roman road – follows the route of the old Chichester to Midhurst railway line, which closed in 1991.

Starting in Chichester, you will pass through Brandy Hole Copse, sixteen acres of managed woodland – mainly sweet chestnut trees – which was made a Local Nature Reserve in 2001.

Look out for the many eye-catching sculptures relating to aspects of local history that have been installed along the way, including one where the Roman road crosses the path.

Earlier human activity in the area is evident in the Iron Age earthwork bank known as the Devil's Ditch, the line of which crosses the path south of Mid Lavant. This is thought to have enclosed a high status settlement on the coastal plain to the south.

Distance: 5½ miles (8.8 km)
Time: 45 minutes cycling / 2 hours walking (non-circular)
Terrain: No stiles. Suitable for cyclists and walkers. Flat and wide path with minor slopes
Start: Near Bishop Luffa School, Chichester (SU847047)
Nearest Postcode: PO19 3JT
Map: OS Explorer OL8 Chichester

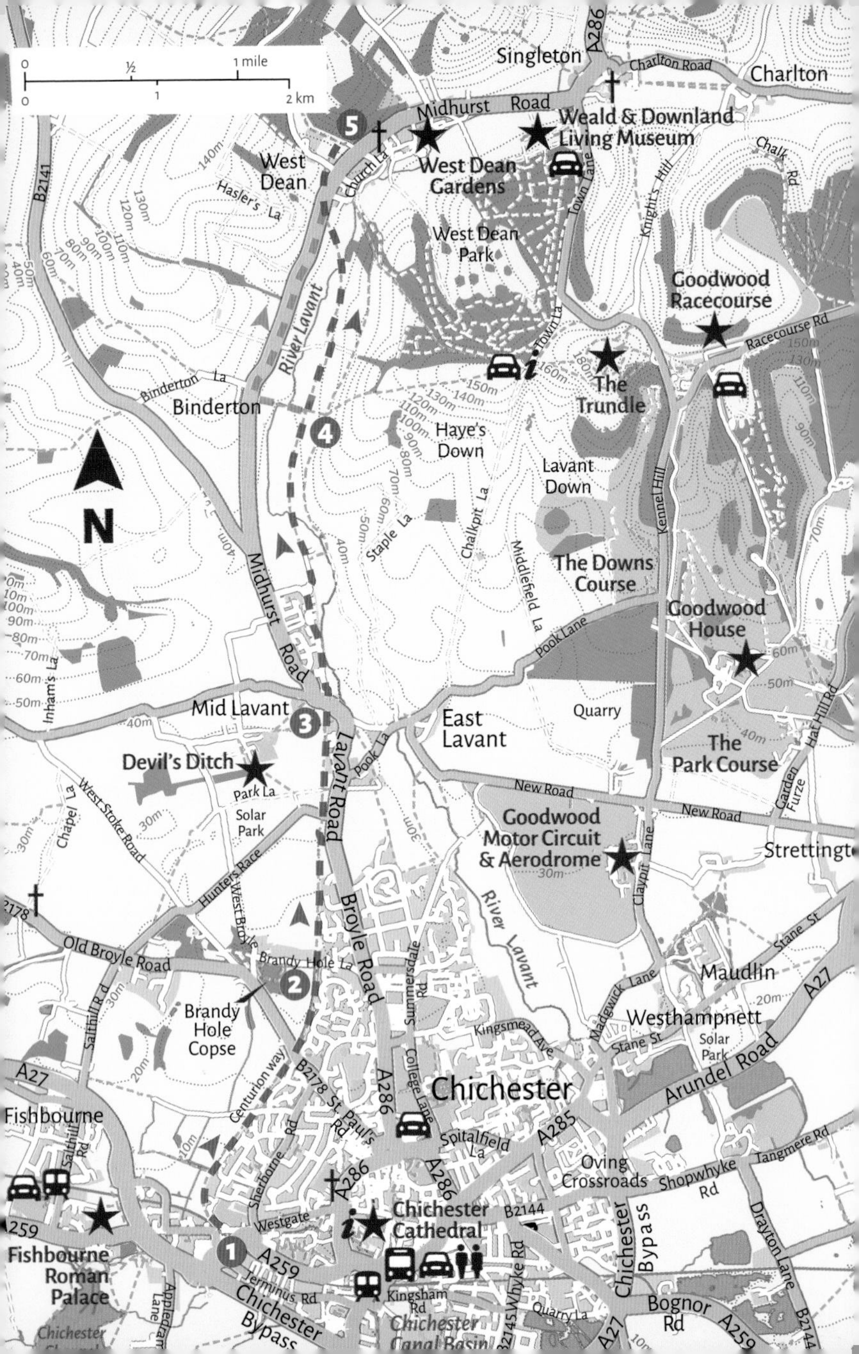

0
½
1 mile
1
2 km
N
Singleton
Charlton
Charlton Road
A286
Midhurst Road
Weald & Downland Living Museum
West Dean Gardens
West Dean
West Dean Park
Church La
Hasler's La
Town Lane
Knight's Hill
Chalk Rd
Goodwood Racecourse
Racecourse Rd
The Trundle
Town La
River Lavant
Binderton La
Binderton
Haye's Down
Lavant Down
Staple La
Chalkpit La
Middlefield La
Kennel Hill
The Downs Course
Goodwood House
Pook Lane
Midhurst Road
Mid Lavant
East Lavant
Quarry
The Park Course
Devil's Ditch
Park La
Solar Park
Pook La
Lavant Road
New Road
Goodwood Motor Circuit & Aerodrome
Claypit Lane
Strettingt
Hat Hill Rd
Garden Furze
West Stoke Road
Chapel La
Inham's La
Hunters Race
West Broyle
Old Broyle Road
Brandy Hole La
Brandy Hole Copse
Broyle Road
Summersdale Rd
River Lavant
Madgwick Lane
Maudlin
Stane St
Westhampnett
Solar Park
Kingsmead Ave
Salthill Rd
A27
Fishbourne
Centurion way
B2178 St Paul's Rd
A286
College Lane
Chichester
Arundel Road
Spitalfield La
A285
Oving Crossroads
Shopwhyke Rd
Tangmere Rd
Sherborne Rd
Westgate
Chichester Cathedral
B2144
Chichester Bypass
Drayton Lane
Fishbourne Roman Palace
A259
Terminus Rd
Kingsham Rd
Whyke Rd
Quarry La
Bognor Rd
Apuldram Lane
Chichester Bypass
Chichester Canal Basin
1
2
3
4
5

❶ To the west of Chichester city centre, join the Centurion Way shared path to the left of the entrance for Bishop Luffa School.

❷ After almost a mile (1.5 km), pass underneath the bridge. The picturesque woodland of Brandy Hole Copse is on your left and can be reached directly from the Centurion Way by exiting the path onto Brandy Hole Lane.

❸ Continue on the path for 1½ miles (2.5 km), passing the Devil's Ditch to your left, to reach the village of Mid Lavant and the former Lavant Station. Follow the signed route through the quiet housing estate for 0.6 miles (1 km), bear right onto Churchmead Close and then right again onto Springfield Close. Continue along Lavant Down Road and pick up the route on the other side of the green.

❹ At the bridge you can either continue straight on following the path to a set of steps to access West Dean, or turn left and follow the segregated path alongside the A286.

❺ After a further 1½ miles (2.5 km) you will reach the turning point at West Dean Tunnel. You can access West Dean village for refreshments via a set of steps and a wheeling ramp for bicycles.

The beautiful West Dean Gardens lie at the northern end of the Centurion Way walk.

WALK 20

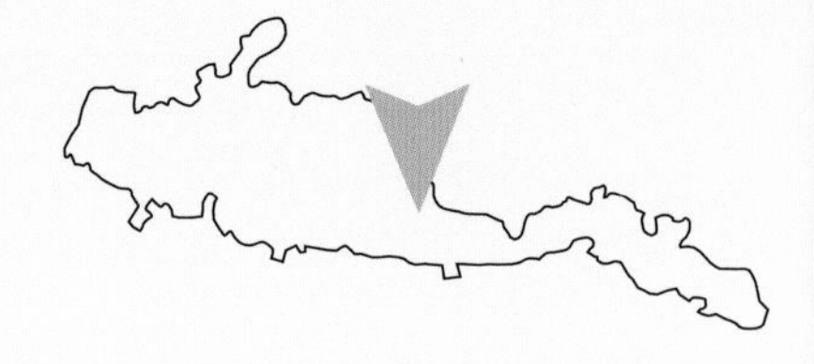

Amberley

This lovely walk has a bit of everything – views, wildlife and history.

Amberley is a chocolate box village which, despite its small size, is packed full of interesting buildings and places to see. As well as thatched cottages and the Norman church, there is a stunning medieval castle (now a hotel), a working pottery and a heritage museum occupying a former chalk pit. Set against the backdrop of the steep scarp slope of the Downs, the village sits on the edge of the sweeping floodplain of the River Arun.

You can clearly see where the river carved out its channel through the chalk. Nowadays flood banks confine what was once a wild and wandering river.

To the north, the flood meadows at Amberley Wild Brooks are an important site for birds – including the rare Bewick's swan – insects and plants, providing something to see all year round.

This circular walk begins at the railway station to the south of Amberley, taking you along the path beside the River Arun and round to explore the village before returning past the museum. There is also an optional extension to visit the nature reserve at Amberley Wild Brooks.

Distance: 2½ miles (4 km) (optional 1.8-mile (3-km) extension)
Time: 1½–2 hours
Terrain: Some stiles. Path can get muddy.
Start/Finish: Amberley Station (TQ026117)
Nearest Postcode: BN18 9LR
Map: OS Explorer OL10 Arundel & Pulborough

❶ From Amberley Station cross over the road to the pavement and turn left under the railway bridge. Shortly after this take the footpath on your right along the bottom of the railway embankment. Follow the footpath along the river bank until you arrive opposite the village of Bury.

❷ Turn right, away from the river, and follow the footpath across some low-lying fields (this section of path can be boggy in wetter months). After crossing the railway line and passing a section of the castle walls you arrive in Amberley village.

❸ Turn left at the junction shortly after passing the pottery.

❹ To extend the walk, take the steep track down to Amberley Wild Brooks before returning the same way. This will give you a flavour of this extensive and important wetland area.

❺ At the junction turn right and walk downhill, past the village shop, and turn right at the next junction just before Amberley Village Tea Room.

❻ You've now arrived back where you were at route point 3 but going the other way. This time turn left and take the footpath opposite the road which will take you past the village recreation ground to the main road.

❼ At the main road turn right along the verge path back to Amberley Station, passing close to Amberley Museum and Heritage Centre (to your left) as you approach the station.

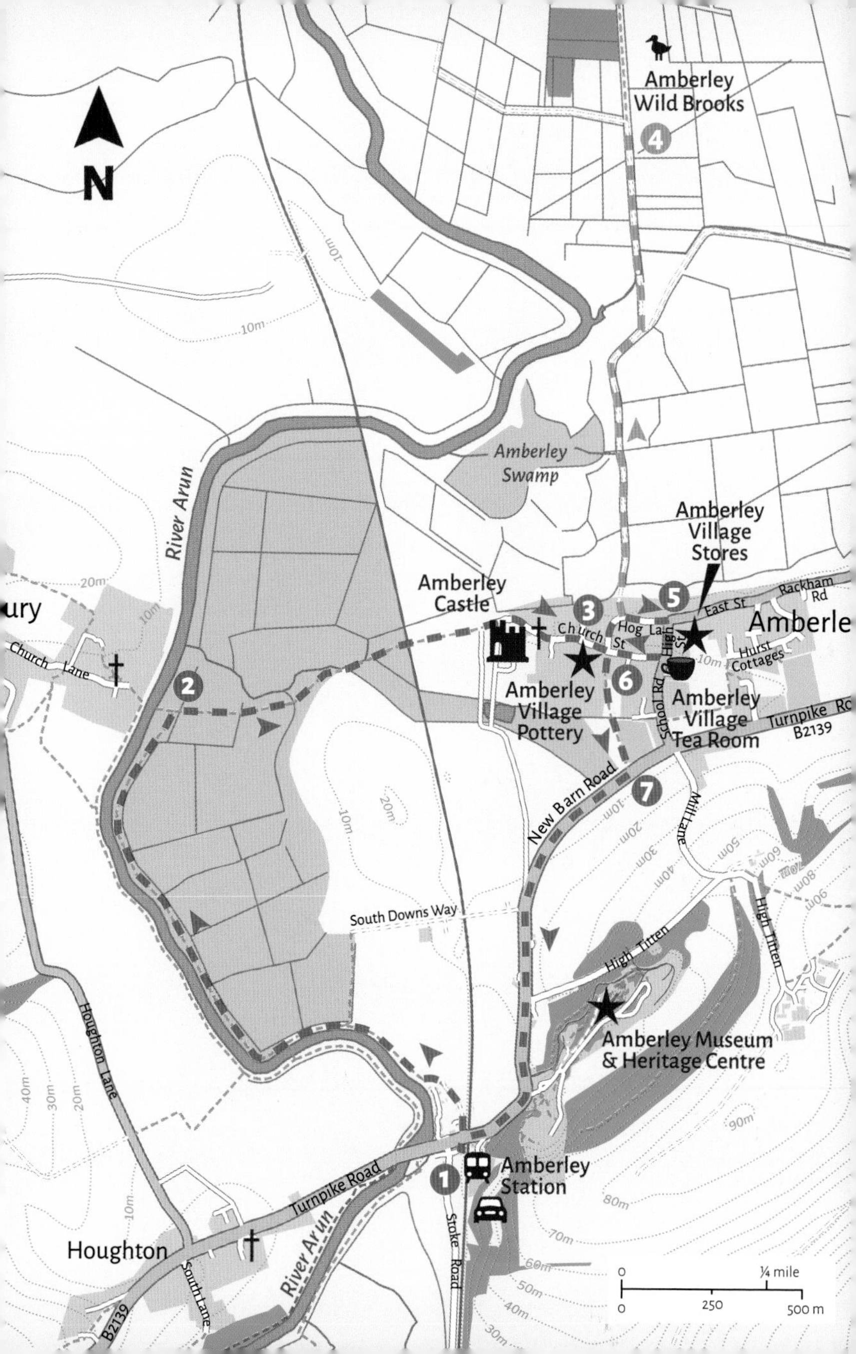

N
Amberley Wild Brooks
4
10m
10m
Amberley Swamp
River Arun
Amberley Village Stores
Amberley Castle
3
5
Rackham Rd
East St
Amberle
Church St
Hog La
High St
Hurst Cottages
6
Amberley Village Pottery
School Rd
Amberley Village Tea Room
Turnpike Ro
B2139
ury
20m
Church Lane
2
New Barn Road
7
Mill Lane
South Downs Way
High Titten
High Titten
Amberley Museum & Heritage Centre
Houghton Lane
1
Amberley Station
Turnpike Road
Houghton
South Lane
River Arun
Stoke Road
B2139
0
¼ mile
0
250
500 m

The imposing curtain walls of Amberley Castle were constructed in medieval times.

Acknowledgements

Thanks to all of the photographers who allowed us to use their imagery in this book.

page 6 © Mischa Haller/SDNPA; 9 © Neil Hulme/SDNPA; 12 © Anne Purkiss/SDNPA; 19 © Daniel Greenwood/SDNPA; 25 © Daniel Greenwood/SDNPA; 28-29 © Sam Moore/ SDNPA; 32-33 © Sam Moore/ SDNPA; 36 © Mischa Haller/SDNPA; 41 © Charlie Hellewell/ SDNPA; 44-45 © Charlie Hellewell/SDNPA; 47 © Anne Purkiss/SDNPA; 51 © Charlie Hellewell/SDNPA; 54-55 © Charlie Hellewell/SDNPA; 57 © Mischa Haller/SDNPA; 60-61 © Colin Carré/SDNPA; 63 © Mischa Haller/ SDNPA; 67 © Mischa Haller/SDNPA; 70-71 © Mischa Haller/SDNPA; 74-75 © Derry Robinson/SDNPA; 79 © Sean Lewis/SDNPA; 85 © Mischa Haller/SDNPA; 91 © Valerie Whittle, Rottingdean Preservation Society; 95 © Warren Peters/SDNPA; 100-101 © 2020 Vision Guy Edwardes; 108-109 © Daniel Greenwood/SDNPA; 111 © Daniel Greenwood; 114-115 © Andrew Pickett/SDNPA; 117 © Anne Purkiss/SDNPA; 120-121 © SDNPA; 123 © Daniel Greenwood/SDNPA; 126-127 Andrew Brownsword Hotels.

SDNPA (South Downs National Park Authority)

Maps © OpenStreetMap contributors
Contains OS data © Crown copyright [and database right] 2020.
Map creation: Cosmographics Ltd (www.cosmographics.co.uk).
Page design and layout: mapuccino (mapuccino.com.au).
Edited by Karen Marland.